EARTH ANGEL
REALMS

ALSO BY DOREEN VIRTUE

Books/Calendar/Kit/Oracle Board

Living Pain-Free (with Robert Reeves, N.D.)

Archangel Daily Messages 2015 Calendar

Angels of Abundance (with Grant Virtue)

The Big Book of Angel Tarot (with Radleigh Valentine)

Angel Dreams (with Melissa Virtue)

Angel Astrology 101 (with Yasmin Boland)

Angel Detox (with Robert Reeves)

Assertiveness for Earth Angels

How to Heal a Grieving Heart (with James Van Praagh)

The Essential Doreen Virtue Collection

The Miracles of Archangel Gabriel

Mermaids 101

Flower Therapy (with Robert Reeves)

Mary, Queen of Angels

Saved by an Angel

The Angel Therapy® Handbook

Angel Words (with Grant Virtue)

Archangels 101

The Healing Miracles of Archangel Raphael

Earth Angels

Messages from Your Angels

Angel Visions II

Eating in the Light (with Becky Black, M.F.T., R.D.)

The Care and Feeding of Indigo Children

Angel Visions

Divine Prescriptions

Healing with the Angels

"I'd Change My Life If I Had More Time"

Divine Guidance

Chakra Clearing

Angel Therapy®

Constant Craving A–Z

Constant Craving

The Yo-Yo Diet Syndrome

Losing Your Pounds of Pain

Audio/CD Programs

The Healing Miracles of Archangel Raphael
(unabridged audio book)

Angel Therapy® *Meditations*

Archangels 101 (abridged audio book)

Solomon's Angels (unabridged audio book)

Fairies 101 (abridged audio book)

Angel Medicine (available as both 1- and 2-CD sets)

Angels among Us (with Michael Toms)

Messages from Your Angels (abridged audio book)

Past-Life Regression with the Angels

Divine Prescriptions

The Romance Angels

Connecting with Your Angels

Manifesting with the Angels

Karma Releasing

Healing Your Appetite, Healing Your Life

Healing with the Angels

Divine Guidance

Chakra Clearing

DVD Program

How to Give an Angel Card Reading

Oracle Cards (divination cards and guidebook)

Angel Answers Oracle Cards (with Radleigh Valentine)

Archangel Oracle Cards
Magical Mermaids and Dolphins Oracle Cards
Messages from Your Angels Oracle Cards
Healing with the Fairies Oracle Cards
Healing with the Angels Oracle Cards

All of the above are available at your local bookstore,
or may be ordered by visiting:

Hay House USA: www.hayhouse.com®
Hay House Australia: www.hayhouse.com.au
Hay House UK: www.hayhouse.co.uk
Hay House South Africa: www.hayhouse.co.za
Hay House India: www.hayhouse.co.in

Doreen's Website: www.AngelTherapy.com

EARTH ANGEL
REALMS

*Revised and Updated Information
for Incarnated Angels, Elementals,
Wizards, and Other Lightworkers*

Doreen Virtue

HAY HOUSE, INC.
Carlsbad, California • New York City
London • Sydney • Johannesburg
Vancouver • Hong Kong • New Delhi

Published and distributed in the United States by: Hay House, Inc.: www.hayhouse.com® • *Published and distributed in Australia by:* Hay House Australia Pty. Ltd.: www.hayhouse.com.au • *Published and distributed in the United Kingdom by:* Hay House UK, Ltd.: www.hayhouse.co.uk • *Published and distributed in the Republic of South Africa by:* Hay House SA (Pty), Ltd.: www.hayhouse.co.za • *Distributed in Canada by:* Raincoast Books: www.raincoast.com • *Published in India by:* Hay House Publishers India: www.hayhouse.co.in

Interior design: Nick C. Welch

Previous editions of this book were published under the titles *Earth Angels* (ISBN: 978-1-4019-0048-9) and *Realms of the Earth Angels* (ISBN: 978-1-4019-1718-0).

Cataloging-in-Publication Data is on file with the Library of Congress

ISBN: 978-1-4019-4562-6

10 9 8 7 6 5 4 3 2
1st edition, December 2014

Printed in the United States of America

SUSTAINABLE FORESTRY INITIATIVE

Certified Chain of Custody
Promoting Sustainable Forestry

www.sfiprogram.org
SFI-01268

SFI label applies to the text stock

CONTENTS

A GENTLE NOTE
TO THE READER

This is not your average book of angel stories, nor is it a book about angels in the ordinary sense of the word. While people usually think of Earth Angels as do-gooders, this work takes the term literally, as you'll soon see. The material within these pages may surprise or even shock those who are accustomed to a more mainstream view of angels.

Some people may mistake this book's intention, thinking that it supports the idea of separation into groups. Yet, what I'm presenting here is merely a description of the personality-related, behavioral, and physical characteristics of Earth Angels, similar to the type of information found in astrology books. Those who are Earth Angels will relate to the concepts in this book; however, others may misunderstand or even object to what I'm offering here. My intention is to help and to heal, but sometimes such actions create controversy.

∝≫∽

Ever since my book *Earth Angels* was first published in 2002, and followed up with a revised edition, *Realms of the Earth Angels,* in 2007, I've had the opportunity to talk to many people about the material. In my certification programs, I discuss the realms in depth and even help my students discover their realm of origin. These studies have yielded additional information about new realms, which are included in this updated and expanded book, *Earth Angel Realms,* and in my video course at www.RealmReader.com.

When I began teaching about the Earth Angel realms, I found that some people couldn't relate to the topic. At first, I assumed that these individuals were "Dabblers," "Shape-shifters," or "Evolvers," meaning that they'd experienced many different realms and couldn't place themselves in just one.

Eventually, I realized that these folks belonged to new, previously undiscovered realms. As we began to identify them, things started to "click" in my research, so this book is the result of my studies into the new realms. I've also discovered additional information about the realms described in the previous two books.

Here, you'll find some of the same material as in the original *Earth Angels* and *Realms of the Earth Angels* books; however, my prayer and intention is that you'll enjoy the new depth of information that has been discovered since my earlier books were first published.

The original *Earth Angels* book included a long quiz to help you discover your realm. In this version of the book, I've replaced the quiz with easily identifiable points at the beginning of each chapter. So, you can quickly scan the first page of each chapter to see which realm you most identify with.

I believe that there are still some more undiscovered realms that will be found in the years to come, so I welcome your input on the topic.

— **Doreen**

All of the stories in this book are true, and all of the individuals whose accounts are included here have given written permission for their stories to be published. The names in the book are also real, with the exception of three people who requested pseudonyms, and two who asked that only their initials be used. I'm very grateful to all of them for coming forward and telling their stories, as they enrich all of us by sharing their experiences.

INTRODUCTION

Are You an Earth Angel?

Do you feel different from other people, as if you were dropped off on this planet and wonder when someone's coming to take you home? If so, then you may be an *Earth Angel,* which is another term for *Lightworker, Star Seed,* or one of the many words used to describe a person who incarnated for the express purpose of helping the world be a better place.

Every person is born with a personal mission to learn and grow. Each of us elects a theme for our life in which we'll work on a particular lesson such as patience, forgiveness, or compassion. Yet Earth Angels also choose a *global* mission in addition to a personal mission . . . and this global mission is to provide a service to the world.

If you have a passion and talent for healing, teaching, or helping others, yet you yourself have low self-esteem, addictions, weight issues, relationship challenges, and the like, then you may be an Earth Angel. If you're highly sensitive and you abhor violence in any form, then you are most likely an Earth Angel!

Although all souls originate from the same Divine source, our environment and personal history often shape our personalities and physical characteristics. For instance, those who spend most of their time surfing at tropical beaches will have different looks and mannerisms than people who work in their inner-city offices every day.

Similarly, all of the lives you've previously lived have impacted you. And, just as your physical family-of-origin influences you, so does your soul's realm-of-origin shape your looks, behavior, and even your life purpose. Again, the *inside* of everyone is the same: a beautiful, pristine spark of Divine light. However, as a lightworker, *your* spark of light may have spent time in heavenly realms far from Earth. Those lifetimes that you've logged in the angelic realm, in the elemental kingdom, or on other planets have influenced who you are today. Although you inhabit a human body, your soul feels like a traveler in a foreign country—because that is, in essence, what you are.

Not everyone is an Earth Angel, of course—for this role, God called in the most dedicated and brightest sparks of light. Those humans who aren't Earth Angels are living lives purely for their own growth, rest, or enjoyment. They may seem dense or decidedly unspiritual, yet they're Divine sparks of life, too. Their lives have simply been dedicated to human, Earthly concerns.

The Earth Angels' Vital Mission

As an Earth Angel, you're a powerful lightworker with a legacy of healing and miracles behind and in front of you. You accepted your Divine assignment to come to Earth and spread your teachings and healing energies. How has your assignment been so far? If you've had difficulty adjusting to Earthly life, then you'll probably find answers, comfort, and guidance by remembering your spiritual origin.

You may discover that you're an Incarnated Angel or Elemental; a Starperson, whose past lives have been extraterrestrial (ET); a Merperson; a Cherub; an Atlantean; a Leprechaun; a Galactic Knight or Knight

Paladin; or a Wise One, which is a reincarnated Sorceress, High-Priestess, or Wizard. You're a seasoned service worker called into action—an Earth Angel. You may have had past lives on Earth as an Incarnated Angel and Elemental, yet you forgot these incarnations, believing that your past lives were human.

The term *Earth Angels* is not to be confused with *Incarnated Angels,* which is one of the realms of Earth Angels. Incarnated Angels and the other realms are all included under the umbrella term, *Earth Angel.*

I'm frequently asked how the terms *Indigo* and *Crystal* intersect with *Earth Angels.* The answer is that Indigo and Crystal aren't realms. They refer to your energy soul group and your group life purpose. Earth Angel focuses on your individual life purpose. So, you can be *both* Indigo and an Earth Angel, and the same is true for Crystals also being Earth Angels.

By learning about your spiritual realm-of-origin, you'll understand more about your personality, behavior, and individual quirks. This is similar to the way our astrological sun signs group us into meaningful categories.

My Early Work with Earth Angels

I first accessed information about Earth Angels through my private practice, where I gave angel, mediumship, and psychic readings. My clients usually consisted of lightworkers who were procrastinating with respect to accomplishing their life mission.

I'll never forget the first Earth Angel I identified during a session. As I scanned her shoulders, looking at her aura and spirit guides, I psychically saw a large artery-like pole extending upward from her left shoulder. As I looked to see where the pole was attached, I gasped. There, spinning above her, I had a clear etheric vision of a hovering spacecraft! I had never had any interests in UFOs or ETs and actually found the whole subject off-putting. I hesitated to tell this woman what I saw, but I'd learned to trust my visions and to faithfully deliver them verbatim to my clients. I'd found that even if *I* didn't understand the visions, my clients usually did.

So I inhaled deeply and blurted out, "I see what may be a spacecraft hovering above you."

"Oh yes," my client replied matter-of-factly. "It's been with me my whole life." This floored me. Keep in mind that this woman looked like your average girl-next-door. Her communication style was very grounded, and she spoke with the vocabulary of one who was aware and educated. There was no hint of her being spacey.

I listened with an open mind as she explained that the ship was her ever-present guide and protector, watching over her and giving her information when needed. She reported having visited the ship during dreamtime sojourns.

Not long after, I saw several other clients with this same extraterrestrial connection. I've always been one to notice personality and behavioral patterns, so I soon noted that my "Starperson clients" had similar aura colors, facial features, relationship patterns, and life missions.

Discovering the Other Realms

Much of the esoteric information that I receive comes from my own guides and angels, who give me messages while I'm sleeping or during readings or meditations. Through these means, I was told of the other soul-group incarnations to look for in my clients and audience members.

First, I studied the *Incarnated Angels.* These men and women have angelic faces, heavyset bodies, and histories of codependent relationships; apologize and talk a lot; and are perennial helpers. For example, my client Laurie is a quintessential Incarnated Angel. She's a very sweet and attractive blonde nurse with a large, curvy figure and a heart-shaped face. After years of trying to help her alcoholic husband get sober, Laurie finally made the painful decision to divorce him. Now she's searching for a way to transfer her natural healing abilities to a private practice.

I next noticed the group called the *Incarnated Elementals.* My client Jayne is a typical member of this realm. With red hair styled in a pixie cut and a thin, lanky body, Jayne looks like someone who'd wear green elf shoes with curled toes and bell tops. She's a professional dog groomer and an avid animal-rights advocate who broke off her engagement because her fiancé wanted to move away from the mountains where she grew up.

"He planned to move to the city," Jayne explained. "I'd shrivel up and die if I didn't live near nature—especially if I moved to the city, where trees are practically nonexistent."

For many years, I assumed that these categories were the only realms from which Earth Angels originated: Incarnated Angels, Elementals, and Starpeople. When I'd discuss these categories with my spiritual counseling students, about 80 percent of them acknowledged an affinity to one of the three groups. I'd even have the students gather into groups with their spiritual clan members. I'd see them crying, laughing together, and exclaiming, "Really? You, too? I'm just like that!" as they swapped stories of Earth life from the perspective of their realm.

But there were always some students who couldn't relate to any of the categories. "What about us humans?" they'd ask.

My son Grant finally supplied the answer. He was attending my Angel Therapy Practitioner® certification course in North Miami, giving a brief talk to the class about using candles in manifestation and healing. Grant had been studying spirituality for some time, and he had a wealth of knowledge to share. At the end of his talk, he turned to the audience and said, "I know what the fourth realm of Earth Angels is. . . . I know, because I'm from this category. It's those of us who are Reincarnated Wizards, High-Priestesses, Witches, Knights, Sorcerers, and Sorceresses."

A collective gasp rose from the audience, followed by exclamations of "Yes! That makes so much sense!" and "That's what I am!" Grant's assessment rang true, and it struck a chord with the class participants.

Since then, I've studied and interviewed many people from this group, whom I now call the *Wise Ones.* Whenever I lecture or write about the topic, I receive confirmation that this powerful group of lightworkers relates to this category. (Since that time, we've realized that knights belong to a separate realm, as you'll read in this book.)

Phyllis typifies the members of this group whom I've met and interviewed. She has an oval face and large eyes, and her faraway stare speaks of someone who sees beyond the physical universe. She wears her hair long; and she has an elegant, almost regal, demeanor. When Phyllis saw the movies *The Mists of Avalon, The Lord of the Rings,* and *Harry Potter and the Sorcerer's Stone,* she immediately related to the ancient, magical skills as ones she'd once possessed. Phyllis also knows that she was burned at the stake for being a witch in a prior life.

My original teachings included a fifth category called "Walk-Ins." These are souls who electively take on an adult body so that they can fulfill their life purpose without having to endure childhood and adolescence. While Walk-Ins are highly evolved souls who are serving very important missions, I've realized that they aren't really an Earth Angel realm of origination. Instead, Walk-Ins are a process. For that reason, they aren't included in this book.

This work includes the new realms that I've found since *Earth Angels* was first published. We now have realms and information for many people who were previously considered "Dabblers," "Shape-shifters," or "Evolvers" (the miscellaneous realm categories). I feel that there are many other yet-undiscovered realms that we'll find eventually, as well. Clearly, this is a field requiring lots of empirical study.

And now in 2014, this third edition of the book contains even more realms that have been identified and studied. In this book, we discuss the newly discovered hybrid realms of Incarnated Cherubs, Atlanteans, Aladdin Genies, Galactic Knights, Mystic Stars, and Cosmic Angels.

In the second edition of the book, there were some complaints and misunderstandings from readers who thought that it would be an entirely brand-new book. Please understand that this third-edition book has the additions of the newly discovered realms and a bit of rewriting. But *Earth Angel Realms* has the same foundational basis of the original book.

The Healing Effects of This Knowledge

When I first began publicly discussing this concept, I realized that I was risking being misunderstood, so I limited my discussions to my certification courses because the students who attended were especially open-minded. Even then, I waited until we were deep into our course to talk about Incarnated Angels, Elementals, Wise Ones, and Starpersons.

Each time I discussed the information, the students expressed tremendous relief, and healing followed. Here is how some Earth Angels surveyed for this book described their reactions to discovering their spiritual origin:

- "Since I found out, I've felt relieved. I no longer feel so strange, and I finally have a sense of belonging."

- "Once I learned about my realm, I realized that nothing was really wrong with the way I acted."

- "It helps me to know that I'm not the only one feeling this way."

- "I've always known that I was different, and now there's an explanation that makes sense."

- "Finally, I realized why I had to help people at all costs. I never knew why I had this drive before."

This healing effect, along with my own guides' urgings and ongoing feeding of information, encouraged me to continue studying this phenomenon.

I had started to write this book several times, yet the moment never seemed quite right—until now—to discuss this topic so openly. I wrote on the subject in one chapter called "Incarnated Angels, Elementals, Walk-Ins, and Starpeople" in my book *Healing with the Angels*. I also wrote an article on the topic, which was reproduced in several metaphysical publications and on my website (www.angeltherapy.com). The chapter and article attracted a great deal of attention; and at every lecture, audience members requested more details, or asked me to identify their Earth Angel realm.

My former executive assistant, Bronny Daniels, identified herself as a Starperson the first time I delineated the categories. (Like many Starpeople, Bronny is a Reiki master.) She resonated particularly with the Pleiades (a star cluster in the Northern Hemisphere), and told me that she twice had spontaneously channeled the Pleideian language. Bronny also strongly suggested that I write this book, and her request ultimately motivated me to do so, since it finally felt like the right time.

I wrote a proposal for the book, which I submitted to Hay House, my publisher, and I was told, "We'll talk about it at our upcoming meeting." I started to wonder if this topic might be too weird for them to consider. Bronny and her Starperson friends prayed that Hay House would agree to publish *Earth Angels.* Not only did Hay House say yes, but they also agreed to publish the updated version, *Realms of the Earth Angels,* and the further updated and expanded edition that you hold in your hands!

Our next step was to survey people who related to the topic of the various Earth Angel incarnations. I first queried my newsletter subscribers, Bronny's Starperson friends, and those who had completed my Angel Therapy Practitioner program. I figured that I would receive a dozen or so completed surveys. Was I ever surprised to discover that the survey was passed around the Internet, and that I received hundreds of responses!

Since the publication of the earlier editions of this book, I've received even more comments and letters from people who relate to this material. They say that the book has helped them to understand themselves and other people. And that was always my prayer!

In 2014, I decided to teach people how to give a "Realm Reading" to discern another person's Earth Angel realm. The video series called "Certified Realm Reader" was created and is now available at www .RealmReader.com.

Characteristics of Earth Angels

There are characteristics that apply to all of the Earth Angels. The chapters in this book describe each realm's individual distinctions, as well as the common denominators that apply to them—including the following:

— *Feeling different, separate, or alienated from others.* Just about every Earth Angel whom I've met, interviewed, or surveyed has said that they feel "different from others." For all of the realms but the Wise Ones, this characteristic continues into adulthood. Wise Ones, because of their multiple lifetimes on Earth, feel comfortable here . . . even under harsh circumstances. Wise Ones know they are different from other humans, and the other realms feel even more alienated from the human race.

Kelly, who is an Incarnated Angel, describes the feeling in this way: "I feel like I don't fit in. I always felt that I was a social outcast. When I was in grade school, the other children told me I was weird. I used to take it extremely personally, and think, *Nobody likes me.* I would sit and cry for hours. I felt so helpless and sorry for myself because I didn't know why they perceived me as being different.

"I was determined to fit in, and I wanted so badly for everyone to love me. But the only thing that really helped me feel like I belonged was to do things for other people. Later, I became aware of how many people were taking advantage of my niceness.

"Now that I understand my origin as an Incarnated Angel, I'm able to look at situations with a different perspective. It's okay to be different. It's okay to be me. This is how I'm supposed to be. Now I don't have to do things for people to make them like me."

Many Earth Angels have been teased or verbally abused because of their different appearance, interests, and behavior. As Terry, a Starperson, recalled, "My sisters always introduced me as 'the one who was dropped off by a UFO.'" Now Terry realizes the kernel of truth in her sisters' taunts, and their words no longer sting her.

— *Intense sensitivity to other people, chemicals, or violence in any form.* Earth Angels from all realms have difficulty being in crowds, feeling bombarded by the overwhelming emotions and physical sensations emanating from other people. Most Earth Angels have learned to avoid harsh chemicals in their food, cleaning supplies, and toiletries due to allergic reactions. Violence in any form repels Earth Angels, including arguments, negative media reports, and violent movies. People often tease them for this trait, saying, "You're just too sensitive!" Yet, this sensitivity is a sacred gift that Earth Angels bring to this planet, enabling them to intuitively know where their services are needed. They couldn't turn off their sensitivity if they tried!

Earth Angel Shelly says, "I've always disliked being in crowds, and in places where there's noise and chaos. Quite often, my level of empathy is more of a problem than a blessing. I often feel scattered and disoriented at the slightest rise in energy. I have difficulty living with other people, so I do best when I live alone."

— *A strong sense of purpose.* Even if the Earth Angel doesn't specifically know what his or her purpose is, there's a sense that the mission involves teaching and healing others. As an Incarnated Angel named Stav put it, "I've always known that my life's mission was to teach, heal, and serve, and to do my part in helping out our troubled world. Although I'm not sure what I signed up for, I'm willing to help."

— *A history of frustrating relationship patterns.* Earth Angels are often raised by emotionally un-available or abusive parents. The reason? Prior to their incarnation, Earth Angels volunteer to bring love and healing to dysfunctional families. Some Earth Angels are "sent" to these families as children to act as healing catalysts. These young Earth An-gels feel like adoptees, since they don't relate to their parents or siblings at all. And truly, these are their *physical* families and not their spiritual families.

Other Earth Angels sign up for challenging family situations so that they can progress extra fast during one lifetime. They literally are angels in families who need them. Unfortunately, the families that need the most love and healing are often the most apt to push it away. Instead of recognizing the angel among them, they are threatened by the light and goodness.

As adults, Earth Angels may attract abusive friends and lovers. Many have romantic relationships with partners who are unfaithful, physically or verbally abusive, drug-addicted, inattentive, or non-committal. Only a strong focus upon understanding and healing this pattern can break the spell cast over their subsequent relationships.

— *Strangers telling them their problems, as well as really personal information.* Earth Angels have lifelong histories of being approached by total strangers who ask for help or divulge intimate details about their lives. People often tell Earth Angels, "There's just something about you that I can trust."

Alisann says, "This has happened to me all my life. I can be standing in a room full of people, and someone will come over and tell me their most intimate information, without my asking them to." This tendency is especially true among Incarnated Angels, as members of the other Earth Angel realms have learned how they can use their body language to discourage this practice. Plus, Incarnated Angels love to engage in long and heart-centered conversations.

— *Looking younger than their chronological years.* Perhaps it's because they eat more healthfully, exercise, and take care of themselves better overall—or maybe it's their spiritual outlook—but Earth Angels often appear younger than their chronological age. Nearly every Earth Angel surveyed reported that people are shocked when they discover their true age. One Earth Angel said that she was carded for buying alcohol until she was well into her 30s. The exception is Wise Ones, whose hair often grays prematurely and whose somber facial expressions, bags beneath their eyes, and body posture can look more mature than their chronological age.

— *Possibly having a history of personal and familial addictions.* Some Earth Angels turn to outside substances or influences—whether food, drugs, alcohol, cigarettes, relationships, or all of the above—to numb the pain of feeling different and of being intimidated by their life mission. One Earth Angel described it in this way: "I found it much easier to cope with life when I used drugs and alcohol. These substances brought me a lightness, or a feeling of numbness, to allow me to forget why I was here. The drugs would put my mission on the back burner. It was more of a worthiness issue back then."

— *A ringing sound in one ear.* Most Earth Angels (although not all) notice a high-pitched ringing sound in one ear. The sound may accompany stressful situations or come out of the blue. Medical reasons for this sound (such as grinding the jaw) have been ruled out. Many Earth Angels consider this sound an annoying distraction, but the ringing is actually encoded information downloaded from the Earth Angels' realm to help them rise above Earthly problems. It also includes instructions and guidance for the Earth Angels' mission. Fortunately, Earth Angels can mentally ask heaven to reduce the volume or pitch of the sound so that it no longer hurts their ears.

This is a book for and about *you!* My prayer is that it will help you heal wounds you may have suffered as a result of feeling different; being highly sensitive or extremely creative; or fitting outside the parameters of norms, expectations, and organizations.

How to Know What Realm You're From

Each chapter describes one or more of the known Earth Angel realms. Read each chapter to uncover which realm you may originate from. Pay attention to your body's signals such as chill bumps, muscular responses, or a sense of *déjà vu*. If you find yourself relating to more than one realm (or none of them), you may be from an as-yet-undiscovered realm or from a blend of two or more realms.

Each realm has unique eye characteristics, so this is one way to distinguish someone's realm of origination. You can also ask your open-minded friends to help you determine your realm. In addition, graduates of my Angel Therapy Practitioner, Certified Realm Reader, and Angel Intuitive® programs can give you educated guidance about the realms. Some of them even teach workshops on the topic.

No matter what realm you're from, you're a beloved child of the Creator. You, like everyone, have an important life purpose, and I'm very glad that you elected to incarnate on Earth at this time!

PART I

THE CORE REALMS

In this section, we'll examine the core Earth Angel realms: those of the Incarnated Angel, the Incarnated Elemental, the Starperson, and the Wise One. These basic realms—which give way to the hybrid realms, discussed in Part II of this book—have straightforward definitions, and aren't blended with any other realm. They stand alone, with distinguishing features that clearly differentiate them from other realms.

CHAPTER ONE

Incarnated
Angels

You are likely an Incarnated Angel if you:

- Have pure and unconditional love in your heart for others (you often exclude yourself from this love, however)

- Struggle with your weight

- Have a beautiful heart-shaped face (even if you believe you need to lose weight)

- Have eyes that shine with pure love

- Frequently lighten your hair color

- Love angels!

- Are talkative

- Frequently are told by others, "You're such an angel!"

- Prefer to know what the rules are, and you always follow the rules

- Work (or want to work) in a helping profession, such as nursing, flight attendant, social worker, teacher, etc.

- Have a history of dating or marrying partners who needed "fixing"

- Apologize a lot, and carry guilt and worry

- Stay in toxic relationships much longer than anyone else would

Reports of Incarnated Angels date back at least to the time of Apostle Paul, who wrote to the Hebrews: "Do not forget to entertain strangers, for by so doing some have unwittingly entertained angels." My books *Saved by an Angel* (Hay House, 2011) and *My Guardian Angel* (Hay House, 2007) include stories of people who have encountered humans who are Incarnated Angels.

Some angels briefly take on human form to prevent a tragedy, and then vanish without a trace before the humans involved have a chance to say thank you. Yet, there are other Incarnated Angels who elect to live their entire lives in a human body—and they're probably among the dearest lightworkers imaginable.

> When you look into the eyes of
> an Incarnated Angel, you see sweet,
> pure, unconditional love.

As mentioned in the Introduction, each realm has unique eye characteristics. The Incarnated Angels have pure, sweet innocence in their eyes. They radiate unconditional love, much like a baby deer's eyes.

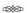

I'm often asked about *Reincarnated Angels*. The term *Incarnated* is more accurate, though, than *Reincarnated*. An angel may have lived more than one life in human form, but if her most recent lifetime was angelic, the telltale characteristics underscore her true spiritual origins.

Many Incarnated Angels struggle with health challenges, especially fibromyalgia, chronic fatigue syndrome, breast issues, and gynecological problems. Louise Hay, the author of *Heal Your Body* (Hay House), says that female health issues stem from "denial of the self and rejecting femininity"; and that fibroid tumors and cysts come from "nursing a hurt from a partner, and a blow to the feminine ego."

These symptoms could apply equally well to male and female Incarnated Angels, who often help others so much that they neglect their own health and other personal needs.

My experience with clients who suffer from gyne-cological, breast, and prostate issues is that they suffer from the "women and men who love too much" syndrome. There's really no such thing as giving too much love. However, when a person gives love and *then resents* the fact that it's not appreciated or reciprocated, the stuffed-down anger can manifest in physical symptoms.

Incarnated Angels look past the surface when they meet people and see their inner talents, divinity, and potential. Incarnated Angels share these characteristics with angels in the spirit world, who only focus upon inner beauty, and urge humans to polish their natural talents in order to make the world a better place.

Incarnated Angels often have friends and lovers who mask their potential with addictions. Incarnated Angels take on these relationships as an "assignment," trying to help others overcome their self-doubts and focus upon their strengths and talents. Unfortunately, this often leads to frustrating relationships for both parties. Incarnated Angels feel thwarted in their attempts to heal and fix their partners. And the partners wonder, "Why are you trying to change and control me?" Many Incarnated Angels fantasize that if they did enough for their partners, or gave them enough love, these people would finally heal. This is fine as long as these individuals believe that a need to heal exists—and are *ready* to heal.

Many Incarnated Angels have histories of abusive relationships, so if they hold on to toxic emotions related to this abuse, their bodies naturally protest.

Energy, Weight, and Food

A propensity toward chronic fatigue syndrome provides other clues about the nature of Incarnated Angels, as all of the Earth Angel realms are extremely sensitive to energy. Yet, Incarnated Angels may be especially vulnerable to toxic energies and energy drains because of their "women and men who love too much" predilection. Incarnated Angels are much more people-oriented and more likely to work in a large corporation, compared to the other types of Earth Angels.

Incarnated Angels need to practice energy shielding and clearing techniques, as described in the next section. Otherwise, it's like going out into a blizzard without a jacket. An Incarnated Angel named Kelly says that this practice helped her enormously. She explains, "Whenever a particular co-worker would walk by or stop to talk to me, I would feel absolutely drained. I could swear that he was snatching my energy. Soon afterward, I read about some people having 'hooks' in their energy field, where their energy reaches out and takes your own energy from you. After observing that this was occurring, I used the exercises in the book to protect my energy. Shortly thereafter, this man stopped coming around me."

Taking good care of their energy also helps Incarnated Angels avoid using food to boost their vitality. Many Incarnated Angels are compulsive overeaters, and it's very common for these lightworkers to carry extra weight on their bodies. Yasmin, an Incarnated

Angel, says, "Being a chocoholic provides me with daily, exquisite reminders of heaven; and it's very hard for me to go without chocolate as a result."

Food delivers a way for Incarnated Angels to ground themselves when they feel spaced-out; and it's also an outlet for stress, especially crunchy, salty foods such as potato chips and popcorn.

It seems that the reason so many Incarnated Angels are overweight is not due to overeating, but because they're energetically shielding themselves with fat. They have difficulty losing weight, even with stringent dieting or exercise. This is especially true among Incarnated Angels who are massage therapists, or who are otherwise engaged in healing touch. They absorb their clients' toxic emotions, and their bodies expand like sponges absorbing water.

With their voluptuous bodies, exquisitely beautiful faces, and large hairdos, female Incarnated Angels look like plus-size beauty queens. They're often told, "You have such a pretty face. If only you'd lose weight, you'd be gorgeous!" Actresses Delta Burke and Elizabeth Taylor are examples of Incarnated Angels with these physical characteristics.

Male Incarnated Angels are burly teddy-bear types, such as actor John Goodman; or those with sweet and boyish faces, such as actor John Dye (Andrew on the TV program *Touched by an Angel*).

Shielding

Before you step outside into the rain, you put on your jacket. Well, in a similar fashion, it's necessary to put on your "energy jacket" each time you engage in helping another person. When you open your heart toward others, you're also open to receiving residual fear-energy they may spew in your direction. That doesn't mean you shouldn't help, but it's just like lending a hand to those who have been out in the rain for a while: They may have a lot of mud on them, and it doesn't benefit anybody if that mud transfers to you. In other words, when you help others clean up their thoughts and emotions, they release the toxins, which may splatter on whoever's near—including you, the helper.

Incarnated Angels tend to be the "bleeding hearts" of the Earth Angel realms, and you particularly need to remember to use shielding techniques prior to conducting any healing work. Otherwise, you're liable to put on extra body fat to protect and insulate yourself. The extra fat doesn't necessarily come from overeating, and you'll find that the weight doesn't budge in response to dieting and exercise. However, the padding is a form of protection that you can swap for a layer of protective energy, or *shielding*.

It only takes a moment to energetically shield yourself. Ideally, you would do this before *any* helping/healing session—whether it's a paid or volunteer session is irrelevant. It also doesn't matter whether the person you're helping is a stranger, a client, a family member, or a friend. And it doesn't matter how long the helping session lasts—it could be a brief moment or several days. Whenever you're about to help someone, shield yourself.

Still, if you forget to shield yourself *before* the session, you can still do so at any time *during* the session. It's never too late to shield yourself; however, by then you may have absorbed some psychic debris, so you'll want to engage in *clearing* afterward. (The next section describes this process.)

Just holding the intention to shield yourself with a protective layer of light and energy makes it happen. It's done. You really can't do it wrong, or be denied access to the light or energy shield. Anyone who holds this intention receives immediate results, without exception.

Shielding means visualizing, feeling, and/or thinking of yourself surrounded in a cocoon of light. This light is the essence of angels; and it's a living, loving, intelligent entity that you've called to surround and protect you. Don't worry. This light is always of the Divine Light of our Creator. So-called dark forces don't have this light available to share with others (nor would they want to do so even if they could). So, you can't accidentally call in a lower energy when you shield yourself.

You can shield yourself in various colors of light, depending upon your intention. Again, know that your intention to surround yourself with this light won't be denied. Anyone who asks will receive it (although the ego sometimes tries to convince us otherwise, and please don't listen to that voice!). The different colors include the following:

— *White light:* This invokes the angels around you to surround you without interruption. The angels protect you, and they ensure that you're safe and guarded.

— *Pink light:* This is the light to invoke if you're with a negative person who's obsessed with their problems. The pink light sends loving energy outward toward everyone who talks with you, and simultaneously sends loving energy inward toward yourself. Nothing can permeate this pink shield except loving thoughts and energies.

— *Emerald green light:* See or feel yourself surrounded by this light whenever you want to heal some imbalance in your physical body. Your body absorbs this light wherever it needs healing energy.

— *Purple light:* Imagine yourself shrouded in royal purple light, which elevates your spiritual frequency, enabling you to rise above problems and contact the highest level of Divine guidance. Purple light also deflects any lower energies, entities, or earthbound spirits.

— *Rainbow light:* See or feel yourself wearing a coat of rainbow stripes, which boosts your ability to conduct energy healing work on yourself or others.

You can shield yourself in layers of multicolored light if you choose, in order to invoke all of the beneficial effects of the various colors. For instance, you can visualize a triple layer of light, with white light first for angelic energy, followed by a layer of emerald green light for healing, and then purple light to elevate your consciousness to the highest truth.

You can also use shielding to protect your loved ones, your home, your vehicles, your city or country, and the world. Just use the same methods in order to envision those people, objects, places, or areas surrounded by healing light.

Clearing

It's possible that you'll forget to shield yourself before a session, so you'll want to regularly engage in energy clearing in order to wash away the effects of fear from your own thoughts, or from the thoughts of others. Fatigue is the main symptom of absorbing these lower energies. This type of fatigue doesn't respond to caffeine, naps, or exercise. The sensation of profound tiredness is chronic, because it's coming from sources foreign to your physical body. Don't worry, though . . . you can easily remove the cause, as well as its effect.

After each healing or teaching session, or whenever you feel very tired, use energy-clearing techniques. Your own guides and angels may teach you methods that uniquely suit you, but here are some of my favorites:

— *Cutting your cords:* This is an essential step for all healers and teachers. Each of your students and clients attach etheric cords to you when they believe that they need something from you. Then, after your session, they draw energy from you. They may also send toxic energy through the cords *toward* you. This is a mostly unconscious process, although the cords are visible clairvoyantly, and palpable clairsentiently.

To cut the cords, simply say this aloud or mentally:

"Archangel Michael, please come to me now and cut the cords of fear that are draining my energy and vitality."

If you're truly ready to release these cords, Archangel Michael will instantly fulfill your request. Sometimes people hang on to cords because of an unhealthy "need to be needed." If this is the case, ask Archangel Michael to help you release the fears behind such a desire. (Remember that the archangels can be with everyone who calls on them simultaneously, and that they don't have time or space restrictions.)

— *Taking sea-salt baths:* If there's no ocean nearby to swim in, you can mimic its healing effects by filling your bathtub with warm water and sea salts, which are available at any health-food store or spa. The pure salt draws out toxic energies from your pores. Be sure to choose a brand without artificial colors or synthetic scents so that you don't inadvertently introduce more chemicals into your body.

— *Connecting with nature:* Plants and animals provide a welcome respite from artificial lighting, electromagnetic frequencies, ringing telephones, and pressures from other people. Plants also draw negative toxins out of our mental, emotional, and physical bodies. When you feel tired, take a walk outdoors. Also, keep a potted plant next to your bed so that the plant and its fairies can conduct energy-clearing work on you while you sleep.

Angels and Assertiveness

Incarnated Angels are born to help and heal, and they come to Earth ready to enact this mission. However, this eagerness can create difficulties if it's unbalanced.

For example, Incarnated Angels carry such optimism about (and love for) humanity that they often have difficulty saying no. Assertiveness training from a counselor, class, or self-help book or audio may be necessary, since many Incarnated Angels say no to themselves in the form of self-denial, while saying yes to everyone else.

Incarnated Angels often apologize for asking for help, or don't delegate at all and then resent the fact that no one's helping them and that they have to do all of the work. This can result in a "martyr/victim complex" in which the Incarnated Angels feel like everyone is taking advantage of them instead of realizing they've created the situation. Some Incarnated Angels feel guilty asking for help, even when making the request of their own guardian angels, due to a fear of "bothering" them. Sometimes this fear stems from years of being teased or verbally abused. The Incarnated Angels believe that there's something wrong with them, so they don't believe that they deserve assistance. They may develop a pattern of self-sabotage and push away opportunities.

The way to heal in this area is to reframe the whole topic of "receiving." This means that these angels need to realize that they can give and help others more if they allow themselves to first receive. For example, if they feel compelled to be healers, they may need a healing center, funds for advertising, a computer, or other accoutrements. They may also need extra money to quit a job that takes their time away from their healing practice.

Related to this is that some Earth Angels, including Incarnated Angels, have difficulty accepting money for their healing treatments. This can create a problem in the case of Incarnated Angels who want to quit meaningless jobs on which they're financially dependent. If they'd accept compensation for spiritual healing or counseling, they could afford to quit their jobs and become full-time healers or teachers.

It's important for client and healer to exchange energy during healing and teaching sessions. In other words, the client or student needs to give something back. This could be money, food, services, or a donation to the healer or teacher's favorite charity. Encouraging a client or student to give back is part of the healing process offered by an Incarnated Angel.

Many Incarnated Angels have "giving and receiving imbalances." The Law of Giving and Receiving means that whenever we give, we automatically receive. It's the flow and the core of the Universe. And clearly, Incarnated Angels spend much of their time giving. In fact, most of them work in helping professions, such as medicine, teaching, counseling, or the travel industry. However, they often block the flow of receiving for themselves through self-sabotage, self-denial, and wasteful spending.

Female energy is receptive energy, and when a female Incarnated Angel gives too much, she can become unbalanced with too much masculine energy. This is also true for male Incarnated Angels. Giving continually, without taking time out for themselves, is another reason why Incarnated Angels may suffer from fatigue.

The affirmations to heal this imbalance are: "I receive good graciously," and "The more that I allow myself to receive, the better able I am to help others." If Incarnated Angels would affirm these words repeatedly and adopt the habit of self-pampering, they'd be more open to receiving in other ways, such as accepting help with their mission. Healthy Incarnated Angels realize that they accelerate God's plan of peace if they work as a team, asking and receiving help from each other.

Incarnated Angels feel very comfortable following rules, and they may be afraid of breaking them. They are hard workers, often bordering on perfectionism in their careers. In fact, the surveys submitted for this book by Incarnated Angels were painstakingly neat and well organized, in comparison to surveys submitted by the other realms. These characteristics make it comfortable for them to work in institutional or academic settings. Many Incarnated Angels work for hospitals, school systems, and airlines. Female Incarnated Angels are frequently employed as nurses, teachers, and flight attendants, or any job requiring a loving heart and saintly patience. I've always thought that it was particularly fitting that so many flight attendants are Incarnated Angels, because after all, angels are accustomed to flying!

I've written a book to help all Earth Angels develop an assertiveness in their personal and business lives. Called *Assertiveness for Earth Angels,* it's especially geared toward Incarnated Angels who are afraid of conflict or who feel guilty for thinking of their own needs.

The Personal Lives of Incarnated Angels

Because Incarnated Angels are physically attractive, generous with their time and affection, and have big, loving hearts, they rarely have difficulty attracting romantic partners or friends. Their difficulty is in finding *fulfilling* and *healthy* relationships, however. Incarnated Angels often see their romantic partners and their friends as potential clients whom they can help and teach. They approach new relationships with the question: "How can I help this person?" Relationships are projects to Incarnated Angels.

As mentioned earlier, Incarnated Angels often fall in love with addicts and then try to fix them. In friendships, they often play the role of counselor. For instance, Incarnated Angels may find themselves listening to their friends' problems for hours. When they try to talk about their own issues, the friends suddenly end the conversation. This is another instance in which the Incarnated Angels' lives are unbalanced as far as giving and receiving. Who listens to *their* troubles?

As mentioned earlier, Incarnated Angels may have been "sent" into dysfunctional families as guardian angels. So they may feel entirely disconnected from their birth families and even wonder if they were adopted, as they have nothing in common. These people don't feel like "family" to the Incarnated Angels, and in truth, they aren't. The family members are stranger-souls whom the Incarnated Angels volunteered to help by coming into human bodies and living with them.

With their tendency to see the goodness and potential in others, Incarnated Angels often remain in unhealthy relationships. They stay put well past the time when the average person would have left.

Pamela, an Incarnated Angel, describes her love relationship pattern in this way: "I attract men who have wounded hearts and are in need of healing. I remain optimistic that they'll heal and that my love will transform them, but that doesn't happen. I have a very hard time ending these relationships, and it takes me a long time to process the pain and separation."

Incarnated Angels often commit to relationships quickly; and soon after the first date they may decide to "go steady," get married or engaged, or live with the new partner. Incarnated Angel Elizabeth says, "I always start to get serious with men right away, although there are things that I don't like about them. I have trouble just dating."

Since Incarnated Angels leap before they look in marriage, and also marry for the first time when they're very young, they may develop a history of multiple marriages or marriage-like relationships. Many Incarnated Angels surveyed for this book were on their third or fourth marriage. They had a new husband or wife every ten years or so. Again, think of Elizabeth Taylor as a quintessential example.

Many Incarnated Angels have difficulty ending unhealthy relationships with lovers, friends, or abusive family members. Like compulsive gamblers, they think that if they keep trying, eventually the relationship will pay off. Incarnated Angels live by the Golden Rule and don't want to abandon others—since they have a great fear of being abandoned themselves. They're also reluctant to be honest about their needs and feelings. So, Incarnated Angels suffer silently in a relationship, taking out their unhappiness on themselves. Eventually, they reach the point of not being able to take it anymore. That's when the Incarnated Angel either leaves or pushes the other person away.

Incarnated Angels may have unbalanced and unhealthy friendships, too. Friendships are based upon give-and-take, but these types of relationships are usually one-sided, with the Incarnated Angels always being the helpers and never the "helpees." The Incarnated Angels are supposed to be the strong ones in any relationship; and the "friends" are entitled to unlimited free-of-charge counseling, healing sessions, and psychic readings.

Eventually, Incarnated Angels burn out from this type of lopsided "friendship." They realize that their "friends" have no interest in them, except in how the Incarnated Angels can help *them.* The Incarnated Angels may feel trapped in a mire of guilt, though, as if they're abandoning friends in need.

It helps if Incarnated Angels have support, especially from others who understand. The 12-step groups Al-Anon and Co-Dependents Anonymous both provide wonderful support for Incarnated Angels trying to heal their relationships. Study groups for *A Course in Miracles* are also powerful places to heal from guilt. Incarnated Angels can probably be found at any event or place involving angels, such as angel seminars, angel shops, or book-study groups that are examining texts about these heavenly beings.

Every relationship is an "assignment," with the potential for both partners to learn and grow. No one is a victim in relationships—they're all chosen, either consciously or on a soul level.

Incarnated Angel Nicole says, "I've been in four marriagelike relationships. All of them have been with men who were emotionally unavailable and abusers, cheaters, and drug addicts. Although my friends and family thought I was a victim, I knew that they could never see what I could see in the souls of these men. I knew that on some level, I was helping to raise their vibration.

"My last relationship was the most difficult and painful. One day I was looking out the window and I told God that I could no longer stay in this relationship. In that moment, I heard the angels say to me, 'We know it is painful; please stay a little longer.' I felt completely loved, and had the strength to finish my work with this man. I'm now with a kind man who's on his spiritual path. He knows that I'm an Earth Angel, and he loves me just the way I am."

Spread Your Wings and Fly!

An Incarnated Angel is filled with wide-eyed compassion and love. The reflection of some personal pain is evident in the eyes, but it's outweighed by the look of Divine Love. Incarnated Angels look past the surface and see the potential within each person. In contrast, an Incarnated Elemental's eyes reflect pure, playful mischief; and a Wise One's eyes have the haunted and faraway look of hard-won lessons.

Incarnated Angels have the classic physical features of angels that artists have captured. They look like angels, whether male or female. With their sweet faces and dispositions, people will call them "angel" without realizing the profound truth of that statement. As Pamela says, "Many people have come up to me and said, 'You look just like an angel,' or 'You're so angelic.' Often these are those who aren't familiar with my work or my love for angels." Many people report clairvoyantly seeing large feathered wings extending from the shoulder blades of Incarnated Angels, and a glowing white light emanating from their bodies.

As with the other Earth Angel realms, it's important for Incarnated Angels to let their lights shine, even if they're afraid of ridicule or rejection. One Incarnated Angel said, "There's a part of me that wants to fold my angel wings and hide my true identity sometimes. This manifests as sometimes not doing my healing work or missing deadlines for advertising my practice."

Yet, when Incarnated Angels spread their wings and fly, it's sheer beauty to behold. Incarnated Angel Judi has realized the importance of surrendering all of her fears to her guardian angels: "At this time, I know that I'm definitely on the right path. All of the desires of my heart are being manifested before me now that I've surrendered and released my life to the service of the angels. Nothing can ever take that away from me. My life purpose and my path have never been clearer or more rewarding. I struggled for so many years, and now I feel like I'm floating on a cloud most of the time!"

Life-Path Work for Incarnated Angels

Incarnated Angels are often attracted to the helping professions, and they make wonderful healers and counselors (traditional or nontraditional), schoolteachers, and members of the travel industry. Most Incarnated Angels enjoy one-on-one work more than working with groups or speaking in front of groups. They're very adept at finding their place in large companies, provided that management has a humanitarian work ethic. Incarnated Angels are miserable working for unethical bosses or firms.

Guidance and Suggestions If You're an Incarnated Angel

If you're an Incarnated Angel, you'll have a more peaceful and prosperous time on Earth if you remember to do the following:

— *Shield yourself with energy and light, especially before helping someone.* This will reduce your need to overeat in order to protect yourself with a layer of extra body weight.

— *Wait before saying yes.* Instead of automatically agreeing to every request for help, give yourself time to meditate, and think about whether it's something that truly is part of your mission and your heart's desire. When people ask something of you, tell them, "Let me think about it," or "I'll get back to you on this." These individuals will respect the fact that you're taking care of yourself.

— *Replace the apology habit with positive affirmations.* Incarnated Angels habitually apologize when they've done nothing wrong. This habit stems from the desire to keep everyone happy, even if it means shifting the blame to themselves.

To boost the happiness quotient of yourself and other people, use positive words instead. Adopt the habit of speaking about yourself, others, and situations with uplifting phrases.

— *Engage in cardiovascular exercise.* This helps in stress and weight management and is important for Incarnated Angels' healthy hearts.

— *Balance your giving and receiving quotas.* Be sure to give *yourself* treats regularly.

— *Drop any rules that restrict your mission.* Notice whether you have personal "rules" you follow without question, such as, "I better not get too successful, or people will be jealous of me and feel pain from this jealousy." Question rules by asking, "Is this rule working *for* my mission or against it?"

— *Delegate.* Ask for help without apologizing.

— *Accept good graciously.* Allow people to give you assistance, presents, and compliments.

— *Play.* Allow your inner child plenty of time to be silly, free, and creative.

INCARNATED ELEMENTALS

You're probably an Incarnated Elemental if you:

- Care deeply about the environment

- Would prefer the company of animals instead of humans

- Get extremely angry at people who are abusive to animals or the environment

- Have a history of excessive partying or addictions

- Have a great sense of humor and are talented at storytelling

- Are a born entertainer
- Never met a rule that you couldn't break
- Love practical jokes
- Rarely feel guilty

This is one of the easiest groups to recognize among the realms. Just as the Incarnated Angels have angelic faces, Incarnated Elementals also physically resemble their namesakes—that is, fairies, elves, pixies, gnomes, incarnated animals, and unicorns. And in addition to the guardian angels that we all have, this group has fairies as their protective spirits.

Very often, members of this group have reddish hair (whether it's full-on red, auburn, or strawberry blonde); and a Celtic heritage or appearance, such as a ruddy complexion or freckles. The exception is the Flower Fairies, who usually have silky, straight hair, either black or dark brown . . . and sometimes blond.

Angel or Elemental?

Perhaps you saw something of yourself described in the previous chapter about Incarnated Angels. Still, you identify strongly with the descriptions of Elementals. If you're confused about whether you're an

Incarnated Angel or an Elemental, here are questions you can ask yourself to help you distinguish between the two realms:

1. How do I feel about rules? If you're an Incarnated Angel, you usually obey rules and get angry at people who break them. However, if you're an Incarnated Elemental, then you can't stand rules and think that people who abide by them are wimps. To an Incarnated Elemental, getting away with breaking the rules is the height of fun. That said, Incarnated Elementals are often caught in the act of rule-breaking, as their playfulness leads to miscalculations. The exception is the Flower Fairies, who are the angels of the Elemental realm, as described later in this chapter.

2. Is there mischief in my eyes? Elementals are fun-loving beings, often practical jokers, and are always looking for a laugh. Incarnated Angels tend to be serious and polite. If you wonder whether you're an Angel or an Elemental, ask a close friend if you have here-comes-trouble eyes. This is a characteristic unique to Elementals. (If you vacillate between being "naughty" and "nice," then you may be a MerAngel, which is a hybrid blend of the Angel and Elemental realms discussed in Chapter 12.) If you're sweet and angelic, you may also be a Flower Fairy, as described later in this chapter.

> When you look into the eyes of an Incarnated Elemental, you see twinkles of mischief or playfulness.

3. What type of wings do I have? Angels have feathered wings, while many Elementals have butterfly or dragonfly wings. The wings are etheric, not physical.

To determine your wing type, either consult an Angel Therapist, or go within and feel for yourself. Focus upon your shoulder blades and feel or see (in your mind's eye) whether the wings are large, feathery, swan-like appendages, or more like buzzing and beautiful butterfly or dragonfly wings.

4. What's my body type? Incarnated Elementals have slim bodies, fast metabolisms, and sensitive nervous systems; while Incarnated Angels have voluptuous bodies, slow metabolisms, and mellow personalities. The exceptions are MerAngels, who are voluptuous hybrids of both the Angel and Elemental realms, and are discussed in Chapter 12; and Star Fairies, who are tall and large framed, as discussed later in this chapter. Incarnated Angels are physically large people and often tall. Incarnated Elementals tend to be petite in stature.

5. What is my relationship to addictions? Most Incarnated Angels are codependents, while Elementals are the addicts. Elementals love to party; Angels love to rescue! The exception is that many Incarnated Angels are addicted to food.

6. What is my disposition? Elementals tend to have fiery, passionate personality styles, while Incarnated Angels are patient and calm. The exception is the Flower Fairies, who are shy and sensitive.

7. How do I feel about having an audience? Incarnated Elementals are born entertainers, and they love having an appreciative audience to applaud their talents. Incarnated Angels, in contrast, are attention shy. Angels much prefer to connect one-on-one, to engage in deep and soulful conversations about feelings.

Other Distinguishing Characteristics

Sometimes Incarnated Elementals are unsure whether they might actually be from the realm of the Wise Ones. That's because Elementals have ancient histories and relationships with wizards, witches, and sorceresses. So the Wise Ones feel very familiar to Incarnated Elementals. After all, the Elementals were present when the witches were burned at the stake, so they may have residual pain from that era, even though they themselves weren't killed. They may have memories of the burnings and confuse them with their own recollections. The primary difference is that Elementals are much more playful than Wise Ones, who tend to be extremely serious, or even somber or stern.

In fact, Incarnated Elementals sometimes get themselves into trouble with their wacky sense of humor. Their jokes may be ill timed, offensive, off-color, or just plain inappropriate. But one of the Incarnated Elementals' missions is to get the world to lighten up, smile, and laugh—even at their own expense.

In the spiritual Elemental kingdom, the fairies, elves, and others hold nightly parties filled with dancing, singing, storytelling, and laughter. They know the spiritual value of playfulness and joy! Not surprisingly, their human counterparts also know how to enjoy themselves. Incarnated Elementals often become professional entertainers, including comedians, actors, dancers, and musicians. Some examples are comedians Carol Burnett, Ellen DeGeneres, Eddie Murphy, and Red Skelton; actress Julia Roberts; and socialite Paris Hilton.

Relationship Issues for Incarnated Elementals

The Elementals were tired of humans' assault on nature, animals, and the environment. They couldn't make headway as tiny spiritual beings, so they elected to take on human lives and bodies to have more power and say-so in cleaning Earth's air, water, and soil; and in helping the animals.

Truth be told, Elementals prefer the company of animals or plants to people. They feel an innate anger toward the human race for hurting the planet. Spiritual Elementals are said to be vicious pranksters, but they're only mischievous toward humans who show disrespect for the environment. On the other hand, they love to help humans who recycle, use Earth-friendly cleaning products, treat animals kindly, and respect Mother Nature. Some of the Elementals' practical jokes are passive-aggressive, stemming from their lack of respect for humans' wasteful ways.

In relationships, romantic partners are attracted to Incarnated Elementals because of their comedic, musical, or artistic skills. But after the relationship begins, Incarnated Elementals may be accused of being "bratty," "immature," "noncommittal," or "stubborn." They exhibit the same personality traits as tiny elves, fairies, gnomes, and the like. In the spiritual Elemental kingdom, these beings are often flirtatious and promiscuous. Incarnated Elementals may exhibit these characteristics in their relationships as well.

The Elementals are much less people-oriented than Incarnated Angels. They like to associate with others so they can party, but then they want to be left alone afterward. Elementals are also prone to substance abuse and addictions. So, in essence, while Incarnated Angels marry addicts, Incarnated Elementals *are* the addicts. The exception is the shy Flower Fairies, who are more like the Incarnated Angels in their natural sobriety.

Many Incarnated Elementals are in helping professions involving people, but usually because they have a "calling" to do so. Like the Hobbit Frodo in the book and movie *The Lord of the Rings,* Incarnated Elementals are reluctant heroes who help people because they *have to,* not necessarily because they *want to.*

They need a lot of space and alone time, especially outside in nature. Elementals can be shy and very private, even though they're extroverted in social gatherings. They appear to be very open about their private lives, yet there's a guardedness that keeps them from revealing their deepest secrets unless they absolutely trust a person—and that's very rare. They may have an "off-with-their-heads" policy about people in their lives. In other words, when Incarnated Elementals are done with a relationship, they're *really* done.

Incarnated Elementals have learned how to signal people when they don't want to be bothered. Evie speaks for many Elementals when she says, "Strangers used to come up to me and tell me their troubles, but I closed off a bit over the years because I had such a problem taking on other people's stuff."

Incarnated Elementals are clowns when they feel comfortable, especially when surrounded by other fun-loving Incarnated Elementals. In dysfunctional families, they may play the role of "mascot," helping the family cheer up and feel better about themselves. Yet, Incarnated Elementals are also sensitive to disapproval; and so may become introverted, shy, or even reclusive at times when they don't feel socially "safe."

They often turn to drugs or alcohol to feel comfortable in social situations.

Compared to other Earth Angel realms, Incarnated Elementals are a physically robust group, reporting very few health problems, perhaps because Elementals are more apt to spend time outdoors, hiking and exercising in fresh air and sunshine. Or, maybe the Elementals' optimism makes them minimize or deny health concerns. The only noticeable health pattern in the surveys submitted by Incarnated Elementals was a high frequency of depression. This depression could arise from retained anger or sadness toward humans, à la "the tears of a clown when there's no one around."

Several Incarnated Elementals said they had histories of childhood asthma. This corresponds with reports that fairies are sensitive to airborne chemicals and need to avoid pesticides and herbicides in their gardens and foods. It could also be claustrophobia from spending too much time indoors, since the Elemental soul needs healthy doses of fresh air.

Manifestation and Magic

The spiritual Elementals know how to manifest all of their needs. This is one reason why they approach their tasks, like tending to flowers, with playful joy. The Elementals know that hard work isn't a necessity in order to create meaningful results—intention and sincerity are more important.

Incarnated Elementals often eschew hard work, and may be perceived as slackers who favor relaxing instead of working. They unconsciously recall lifetimes in the spiritual Elemental kingdom where they could manifest material resources (food, clothing, gold, housing, and so on) out of thin air.

As a result, many Incarnated Elementals feel off-center in the workaday world of human beings, and they begin to manifest poverty for themselves. Incarnated Elementals seem to either create feast or famine, rich or poor. Incarnated Elementals achieve financial security when they're consciously working a process of manifestation, such as the one outlined in John Randolph Price's *The Abundance Book* or my *Angels of Abundance* book. Then the magic begins! Elementals—like the Wise Ones—have magical manifestation abilities. When harnessed, these abilities can bend time and physical laws, and create rapid manifestations and miracles.

Incarnated Elementals have fairies, elves, or leprechauns with them as spirit guides in addition to the guardian angels everyone has. Incarnated Elementals can call upon these benevolent helpers at any time by thinking the thought, *Please help me!*

Elementals and Nature

Incarnated Elementals are truly people of the earth and her spirit. They have great difficulty being indoors for long. While Incarnated Angels are comfortable working in large windowless buildings, it would be devastating to an Incarnated Elemental. They *must* be outside in nature or they become depressed. The happiest Elementals are those who have outdoor jobs, such as leading nature hikes or retreats; working at plant nurseries; or working as forest rangers, landscapers, or dog trainers, for example.

If Incarnated Elementals must work indoors, they should request the office with a window facing a park or grassy area. Similarly, Elementals are happiest with offices that are crammed with potted trees, plants, crystals, and flowers. Playing recordings of nature sounds, such as singing birds, the ocean surf, rain, and the like is also beneficial. In addition, their offices should sport photos of their favorite pets, and statues of fairies and elves. Aromatherapy with genuine (not synthetic) essential oils of plants and flowers helps Elementals stay connected to Mother Earth when they're indoors. (These oils are available at most health-food stores or metaphysical bookstores.)

During break times, it's a wonderful idea for Incarnated Elementals to walk outdoors, even in inclement weather. Elementals need fresh air more than any of the other realms; and those who work in industrial areas devoid of trees and grass can spend time looking at the cloud formations, since Elementals need visual contact with the beauty of the great outdoors. Nature is their church—it's where Incarnated Elementals feel closest to God.

An Incarnated Elemental named C.C. says: "I get so energized and refreshed in any woodsy, watery spot. I sit under a tree and can feel the good earth energy come right up through my root chakra. I feel safest when I can truly be myself without any interruptions except the gentle touch of a breeze or the sound of birds singing their melodies. The scent of the forest seems to empower me and gives me a natural high. I feel like I can conquer all when I'm there. It's a communion with nature at its best. The warmth of the sun is so healing. It's so special and such a privilege to have nature share her wealth of knowledge with me. I'm able to forget all those mundane, everyday things. I can regroup and recenter. You just can't get that in a populated area, not even in my sacred garden place at home. It's not the same."

Most Incarnated Elementals surveyed could point out specific natural environments where they wanted to live, while the other realms were more flexible about what type of area they resided in. Almost all of the Incarnated Elementals remarked, "I *have* to live in the desert," "I *must* be near the ocean," "I *need* to live in the country," and so forth.

As mentioned earlier, Incarnated Elementals prefer the company of animals, plants, flowers, or nature to that of other people. One Incarnated Elemental recalled her childhood: "I never was the popular one, that's for sure. I loved nature and animals and still do. I spent hours playing under the 17 spruce trees that lined our property. I even counted them every day to be sure they were always there. I preferred nature in my play. I loved babbling brooks and jumping from stone to stone."

Deep down, Elementals are angry at people for being so unkind to the earth and so passive about its cleanup. The exception is if they find an understanding and playful companion, often in the form of another Incarnated Elemental.

Since Elementals decide to incarnate to wield more power in helping the plant, mineral, and animal kingdoms, their life purposes almost always involve environmentalism or animal rights. This might mean teaching these values to others; or through direct involvement in campaigns, research, care, or cleanup.

In fact, it's important for Incarnated Elementals to get involved in some environmental or animal-rights cause or occupation to feel meaning in life. In addition, Elementals feel best about themselves if they take personal steps toward bettering the environment, such as recycling, wearing organic-fabric clothing, being involved in environmental activism, or using Earth-friendly cleaning products found in health-food stores.

When I asked one Incarnated Elemental what she considered her life purpose to be, her reply reflected the sentiments of many of the Elementals I've met and interviewed: "My mission is to teach people about protecting the earth and the creatures who live here. I see difficulty for the planet because of man's greed and self-importance. We must do all we can to save the plants and animals before it's too late. So much has been lost. So much is in danger. Many of our fellow creatures are running out of time because of man thinking that he's better than the other creatures. If we continue to bulldoze and build, throw away and exterminate, we won't be thanked for the wasteland that's left."

Every Earth Angel realm displays high levels of creativity. It's logical, then, that Incarnated Elementals make artistic objects from nature. One Incarnated Fairy told me, "I enjoy using flower pods, leaves, pinecones, nuts, and dried flowers to make decorations and ornaments. I've made miniature habitations and furniture outdoors for the little people since I was a child."

Fiercely Protective of Nature

Since the Elementals are God's "nature angels," it's no surprise that Incarnated Elementals become almost maniacally protective of animals, plants, soil, and water. Many of the Incarnated Elementals surveyed for this book told me that they'd risked personal injury or retaliation in order to protect an animal, tree, or other element of nature.

E.J. writes: "I get angry when others disrespect Mother Earth and her creatures. If, while driving my car, one of my friends throws a cigarette out the window, I pull the car over and make them pick up their cigarette and dispose of it the right way."

Devon (not her real name) recalls: "I was sitting in my beautiful office one sunny day, which has floor-to-ceiling picture windows. I was staring out at the lovely trees, bushes, and rolling hills just beyond the parking lot, and I noticed a strange pickup truck pulling up. A man who didn't work in our building had stopped in our lot to eat his lunch. That was not a problem.

"However, when he threw his tall plastic beverage container into a flowering bush near his truck, it *was* a problem. When I saw this, some type of primal rage boiled in me (I'm normally a quiet, calm, laid-back person). I grabbed a coworker and hissed, 'Come outside with me!' I guess I wanted moral support for what I was about to do.

"I ran out to the guy's truck, yelling, 'What kind of person are you to throw trash into a bush?!' He just sneered at me. I ran down the brush-covered slope (with bare legs) and retrieved the cup, scratching my legs all the while. In a moment of unbridled anger, I threw the cup into the open window of his truck, and yelled at him to leave immediately or I'd call the police. He screeched out of the parking lot, screaming foul epithets at me as he drove away.

"My co-worker just looked at me in shock, as she'd never seen me act this way in the five years she'd known me. She said, 'That's crazy. He could have pulled out a gun and shot you.'

"I realized that she was right, but I didn't care. I would not allow my friend, the flowering bush, to be treated in that way—not while I was a witness to it." I've seen the same vigilance recently with Incarnated Elementals being outspoken leaders of the non-GMO (genetically modified organism) movement.

Pamela recalls: "Around the age of 19, I became aware of being one with nature. I had sprayed a bee caught in the windowsill with window cleaner and was suddenly struck by the thought, *What right do I have to kill it?* I immediately took the bee outside to the front of the house, laid it on the ground, and began to rinse it off with water. My mother thought I was crazy, leaning reverently over a dead bee, trying to resuscitate it. From that point on, I didn't kill bugs anymore. Recently, I gently swept up a swarm of ants in my apartment with a broom and put them outside. Then I politely requested that the ants no longer return, and a week later they stopped coming."

The Different Types of Elementals

As mentioned earlier, Incarnated Elementals look just like their counterparts in the spiritual Elemental world. They are larger versions of fairies, pixies, leprechauns, and so on. Here are some examples of the various types of Elementals:

Incarnated Fairies

Fairies are a subset of the Incarnated Elemental realm, and they could almost be their own realm! Fairies are petite and thin (with the exception of Star Fairies, described below), and they have high energy. Often, their voices are high-pitched. Jenny is a perfect example: she's five feet tall, with a slim figure, a pretty face, large eyes, and long wavy hair that falls to her lower back. Jenny looks like she could be a model for fairy paintings and statues. She is also sweet, unassuming, and shy—just like a fairy. In fact, Jenny is so connected with the fairy realm that she gives professional angel and fairy readings, often using my *Healing with the Fairies Oracle Cards*.

There are dozens of different types of fairies. The various areas where they live and their specialties have strong influences upon the appearance and personality of each different type of fairy. Here are some of the Incarnated Fairies that you're likely to meet (or to be yourself!):

Forest Fairies: Slender, with wavy hair that has red coloring, the Forest Fairies are assertive, strong, and powerful. You might say that they are the Indigo Children of the Fairy Realm, because they are the ones most likely to speak up about crimes against nature and animals. Forest fairies love trees and need to be near them to feel physically and emotionally healthy. They develop special bonds with particular trees, and even have conversations with them. If someone harms a tree, beware because Forest Fairies put their whole energy into protecting trees. Forest Fairies can be tall.

Flower Fairies: Flower Fairies are the sweetheart angels of the Incarnated Elemental realm. Shy and ultra-thoughtful, these fairies are as delicate as flower petals. They usually have flawless complexions and look like petite models. Not surprisingly, they love flowers, and do well in professions involving flowers—such as being a florist, working with essential oils, flower arranging, still-life art, and design.

A high percentage of Flower Fairies are of Asian or Polynesian descent.

Star Fairies: The largest of the Incarnated Elementals, Star Fairies are tall and big-boned. They often carry extra weight, as well. Star Fairies are a hybrid of the Incarnated Elemental and Starperson realms. Star Fairies are socially awkward (like most Starpeople), and they are sweet, kind, and gentle souls. Star Fairies are the elementals who nurture the extraterrestrial flowers and plant life on other planets. They have a natural green thumb born of their innate healing energies, which propel flowers to blossom and plants to grow. Star Fairies do well as behind-the-scene environmentalists, such as working for a nature charity, or as photographers or writers focused on nature.

MerFairies: MerFairies are a hybrid of the Merpeople and Incarnated Elemental realms. MerFairies look like petite and thin mermaids and mermen, usually with a Celtic appearance. They feel a strong connection to all bodies of water, but particularly to lakes, rivers, and streams. MerFairies do well in professions involving wildlife and water conservation.

Pixies, Elves, and Brownies

Evie is a professional singer/songwriter with a ski-slope nose and short dark hair. She says, "People say I look like a pixie. My nicknames when I was young were 'Tinkerbell,' 'Twinkletoes,' and 'Teensy.' I constantly have people come up to me after I've finished singing and tell me they think I'm a pixie, so I think I must be."

Unicorns

Incarnated Unicorns are the ultimate free spirits, who dislike commitments or anything that restricts their freedom. Physically attractive men and women with flowing long hair and slim bodies, Incarnated Unicorns are elusive "prizes" as prospective romantic partners . . . but they don't want to be "caught," so will evade marriage and other commitments. They make wonderful fashion models, as long as the schedule is flexible.

Brian (not his real name) has a protruding jaw, prominent cheekbones, large eyes, and a chiseled face, like an Arabian horse. Brian dresses in long, flowing shirts untucked from his pants, reminiscent of a unicorn's mane, and prefers his hair to be on the longer side. If you look closely at him, you can see or feel an etheric unicorn horn protruding from his forehead. In psychic readings, clairvoyants tell Brian that his spirit guides are unicorns. This doesn't surprise him, as he has always felt an affiliation with this remarkable beast. In fact, Brian has many items that sport unicorn images. His personality is that of a seeker—he goes after spiritually based opportunities and relationships, and magically manifests new doors opening for himself. Brian says that he knows he's an Incarnated Unicorn—the message was given to him by his own guides and angels long ago.

Incarnated Animals

People who have a strong identification with a particular animal may, in fact, have been that animal in a previous lifetime! And in this lifetime, their Divine purpose called them to take on human form . . . but they still retain characteristics of their former animal incarnation. For example, Barbara considers herself to be an "Incarnated Cat." She says:

I feel a camaraderie with cats and plants, and my hair has been a sexy silver color since I was a young woman of 20. I'm surrounded by lots of pet cats, and I communicate with felines and plants wonderfully. I don't especially *like* people, but will help when needed as long as they don't infringe on my quiet, private time.

I have always been a cat. I worship cats and believe that if the energy in the Universe has some type of form, it would be a wonderful catbeing. Like a cat, I'm able to tell if a person is going to perform evil acts—perhaps not specifically what the acts are, but I can feel upon the first meeting if a person has evil or honorable intentions. I want to tell the world that we have to respect one another, the animalbeings, and especially our Earth Mother . . . the environment.

Incarnated Cats tend to be fiercely independent people who need alone space, dislike being controlled, and spend a lot of time grooming themselves. Another Incarnated Animal, the Incarnated Dolphin, is discussed in Chapter 12: MerPeople.

Incarnated Crystals

Not to be confused with the "Crystal Children," who are highly sensitive and psychic youths, Incarnated Crystals are souls who previously inhabited the energy of crystals, boulders, and other mineral elements of the earth. Incarnated Crystals feel very connected to Mother Earth, rocks, and gems. They love to hike and spend time outdoors, and they're very protective of the rock and soil environment. They tend to be large framed, calm, and slow moving.

Life-Path Work for Incarnated Elementals

Incarnated Elementals do well in artistic or media-related careers, including music, film, comedy, writing, publishing, dance, and yoga. Because they tend to be optimistic and are wonderful manifesters, they also make powerful motivational speakers and spiritual teachers. Incarnated Elementals love an audience and do well teaching and entertaining groups of people. They also enjoy nature-related jobs, such as petsitting or grooming; gardening and nursery work; and conservation, environmentalism, and forestry. Incarnated Elementals are natural pet and plant whisperers; they enjoy and do well in related professions, such as dog training or landscaping work.

Guidance and Suggestions If You're an Incarnated Elemental

— *Spend a lot of time in nature.* As I've emphasized repeatedly in this chapter, it's essential for Incarnated Elementals to be outdoors regularly, regardless of the weather. So, if this is your realm, take off your shoes and walk on the grass or soil every day as a way of staying grounded and connected to the earth.

— *Laugh and play.* Elementals who don't play often become depressed. So, look for ways to be silly, have fun, and laugh daily.

— *Manifest consciously.* See yourself as healthy, fulfilled, abundant, and loved. Call upon your counterparts in the spiritual Elemental kingdom to help you manifest your desires. Don't settle for poverty, because you don't have to! You have the magic touch, and can manifest plenty to spare and share with others.

— *Don't throw fireballs.* Elementals' tempers are legendary, and Incarnated Elementals are no exception. When you throw a fit of rage, be careful, because you're energetically throwing fireballs of hot emotion! These fireballs can cause the objects of your wrath emotional or physical pain. Your power is like a volcano when you erupt, so please use caution. Plus, the energy can boomerang and cause painful effects for you. If you find that you've inadvertently thrown a fireball, extinguish its power immediately by calling upon the spiritual Elementals' help.

— *Detox.* You're more effective at manifesting with the high, stable energy of sobriety. You'll also feel happier and healthier with a detoxified mind and body.

— *Engage in environmentalism.* Volunteer your time or give donations to charities involved in cleaning the earth or helping animals. Recycle religiously, and spend the extra money for nontoxic cleaning chemicals, organic food, and environmentally friendly products.

CHAPTER THREE

STARPEOPLE

You may be a Starperson if you:

- Go out of your way to be helpful, and don't want to be thanked or acknowledged

- Love technology and new gadgets

- Are a workaholic

- Adore science-fiction books and movies

- Are fascinated by extraterrestrials and life on other planets

- Have dreams or memories of being on a spacecraft

- Have had encounters of the fourth kind

- Are fairly egoless, and don't think about yourself much

- Are an energy healer

- Got married later in life, or have never been married

- Gave birth to children via C-section

- Are a woman who doesn't like to wear makeup or dress up

- Are more focused on accomplishing tasks than on relationships

- Are socially awkward and don't enjoy small talk

- Find that discussing feelings is unnatural to you

- Are shy and don't like attention called to you

Hollywood films and sensationalistic books portray extraterrestrials as vicious warmongers. Yet, to ETs, humans are the ones who are violent—so violent, in fact, that many ETs were asked to take on human bodies to try to avert mass destruction. We call these benevolent helpers *Starpeople* (or, the singular *Starperson*).

Thank God for Starpeople. They came from physical and nonphysical galaxies and took on Earthly lives to spread kindness on an "as-needed" basis. Their collective niceness helps to defuse the anger, stress, and rage that could lead to destruction. If Earth is destroyed, the negative effects will ripple through many galaxies. The Starperson's assignment, then, is to prevent nuclear war at any cost. The main avenue for this lofty goal is through the expression of kindness and common decency to others—a domino effect of sorts.

On any given day, Starpeople calmly smile as they perform unselfish deeds for others on their path. Those whom they help barely notice them, yet Starpeople don't perform acts of service in order to gain accolades. Such deeds are an innate necessity to them—as if some sort of inner programming compels them to act. They aren't concerned that people rarely thank them.

Starpeople are in any place where kindness is needed. They are grocery-store checkers, postal clerks, bank tellers, and customer-service agents. They are also shy and quiet doctors and nurses who seem to have no bedside manner, because they are completely focused on healing the patient instead of small talk. With their wallflower looks and personalities,

Starpeople prefer to stay "behind the scenes." Their mission doesn't call for high visibility. Quite the contrary: Starpeople are "undercover do-gooders" who hope no one notices them.

This is the first Earthly life for many Starpeople. And because this planet is so violent, emotionally and physically, Starpeople often feel overwhelmed and wish to return home. After all, Earth is one of the most turbulent planets in the Universe, and, in fact, the Universal powers have us quarantined so that we won't harm other planets. Earth is considered as dangerous as a teenager on steroids wielding a loaded gun.

Since it would upset most people to receive direct intervention from ETs—no matter how benevolent they might be—these mighty and gentle beings elected to take on human form and walk among us. On the inside, they're the same as anyone else: beautiful sparks of Divine light made from the same Creator. Yet, because they've spent their lifetimes in non-Earthly locales, Starpeople may seem odd in behavior or looks.

Socially awkward due to their inexperience with Earth life, Starpeople may feel rejected by others. Many of the Starpeople interviewed for this book reported a history of being viciously teased in childhood, and sometimes in adulthood as well. They are misdiagnosed as autistic or having Asperger's syndrome, because they don't know how to engage in normal conversations.

These experiences make Starpeople especially homesick for a planet where they fit in and know the rules of social engagement. Starperson Linda recalls, "When I was a teenager, I used to sit in my front yard and pray for a UFO to come and take me away, to take me home."

In a similar vein, Starperson Scott says, "Metaphorically, I've had my bags packed and have been ready to go home all my life. I'd prefer to work from the other side as a guide. I can remember being on another planet before coming here and being asked to participate in this planet's current drama."

Starpeople often have distinctive physical characteristics that set them apart. Rarely average height, most male Starpeople are tall and thin, with the female Starpeople being small in stature, with either thin or heavyset bodies. Of course, there are exceptions, but in general, the Starpeople's bodies—like their lives—are usually out of the norm in both height and weight.

Starpeople's faces can be long and thin, especially if they have tall, slender bodies. Starpeople who are petite have rounder faces. It appears that the planet of origin may influence their specific physical characteristics.

> Starpeople have unusual-looking eyes, such as an exotic iris color, or uncommonly shaped eyes or eyelids.

Across the board, Starpeople have unusually shaped and colored eyes. It's common for Starpeople to have crescent moon–shaped eyes, like an inverted U. Their eyes are often gray, green, or black-brown, and seem to glow from within, as if they have bright lights behind them. Starpeople may also have rings of lighter color around their pupils.

Since Starpeople don't like to call attention to themselves, they dress for comfort and practicality, instead of for fashion or show. Female Starpeople wear a minimum of makeup and don't like to fuss with their hair. Even a Starperson surveyed who's a professional hairdresser told me that she doesn't spend much time on her own hair color or style!

One sure way to know if a woman is a Starperson is by her eyebrows. Starwomen shave or pluck their eyebrows until they're very thin or nonexistent.

Sometimes they tattoo very thin eyebrow lines. This lends an oddly otherworldly quality to their looks.

Starpeople have paradoxical personalities: On the one hand, they're eager to assist people without being asked, yet they also seem guarded and distant and may be perceived as "cold." They're here to be helpful, without getting involved in feelings and emotions, which are unnecessary to them. Completion of tasks is more important to them than relationship development.

Starpeople love technology, and they're usually the first to own (or invent) the latest devices. They collect state-of-the-art smartphones and tablets, along with other technological gadgets. Part of their collective soul purpose is to further technological ingenuity, for the advancement of science and humankind.

Interestingly, there aren't as many celebrities from this realm because of Starpeople's love of staying behind the scenes. A Starperson would be more likely to direct a movie than star in it. Yet, Oprah Winfrey and Keanu Reeves are reputed to be Starpeople with high-minded purposes who are using the media as their vehicle to teach. Many believe that the film *The Matrix,* starring Reeves, contained a timely message warning us of technological dependency.

Many Starpeople wonder what their life purpose is and are relieved to find out that it involves being helpful on an ongoing and nonspecific basis—in other words, to help in whatever way is necessary. There is no one "job" or "task" that they need to perform during their lifetimes as long as they're doing their best to transform human frowns into smiles.

Starperson Kath says, "It feels as if I was placed here to help anyone or anything that needs my assistance. Not a day goes by without someone needing my help in one form or another. It has been frustrating because I've never felt like I had a 'true purpose.'" Kath was relieved to discover that her continual acts of kindness and helpfulness *do*, in fact, represent her purpose.

Connections with Home

Most Starpeople have interests in UFOs, life on other planets, space travel, and ETs. They love the *Star Trek* TV series (both old and new versions), works of science fiction, and anything else that relates to these themes and topics. They completely relate to the movies *K-Pax* and *Man Facing Southeast*, two films about Starpeople in human bodies who were diagnosed as delusional because they spoke the truth about their non-Earthly origins and who were put into mental institutions.

As children, Starpeople find that they have an intuitive understanding of spirituality. Many of them eschew traditional religion because it seems too restrictive compared to their understanding of the vastness of Spirit. Starperson Terry says, "I always thought of God as a Universal Intelligence that is way bigger than what conventional churches made claim to." This wisdom was most likely gained from many lifetimes of high-level awareness and experience.

Many Starpeople recall being aboard a spacecraft in this lifetime. Several of the Starpeople surveyed even knew their planet of origin. Of course, this isn't material normally discussed in polite company. Remember that these are very ordinary-looking people who know that they aren't from Earth. They're everyone's next-door neighbors, co-workers, mild-mannered doctors, and such, which makes reading their stories even more fascinating. Here are a few of them:

MaryKay: "Through guided visualization, I was taken on a trip to find my home. Jesus came forth as my guide. We went deep into the earth, then all of a sudden, we were up in the sky. We ended up at a really bright star, so bright that I couldn't see anyone. There, I felt the love I'd been searching for my entire life. When I asked where I was, I immediately heard the word *Sirius* . . . and I had never heard that word, or that star, before."

Linda: "I've always felt like I came from Pleiades. I don't even know how to spell it. As to why I feel like I come from there, I don't know why. It's just a feeling I have."

Scott: "I know that I spent my last lifetime on a planet call Zeron. As best I can recall, I tended the forests there. I had a rather large head and was very tall. It was a planet to go rest and relax between lessons. It was very beautiful and green, quite lush. I was having a good time there." In his Earthly life, Scott is a landscaper.

Beings who live on other planets have much longer life expectancies than Earth beings. This is due to physiological differences. In addition, they don't undergo the stress, pollution, and toxic diets that damage Earthly human bodies.

Many ETs have nonphysical bodies on other planets because that's what's best for their mission at that time. Left-brained scientists believe there's no life on other planets, because they are only focused on seeing carbon-based human bodies. They don't realize that life-forms are different for each planet, and may not be apparent to the human senses. But the main reason why beings on other planets have extended lives is that the longer someone lives, the more can be learned.

So, a lifetime on another planet might equate three or four lifetimes here on Earth. That's why some Starpeople choose to have two or more Earthly lives during their "assignment" here. They're still Starpeople because most of their souls' history has been spent on non-Earthly soil.

When Starpeople undergo a past-life regression, the memories may not be their own. Author and past-life regressionist Dolores Cannon made this remarkable discovery while working with a client named Phil. During regressions, Phil recalled various Earthly lives. Then he remembered being on a planet quite different from Earth.

Through a series of regressions, Dolores found that this was actually Phil's first lifetime on Earth. However, he "borrowed" past-life memories from a sort of spiritual library. These borrowed memories of other Earthly lives helped to insulate and buffer Phil as he adapted to the harsh and dense Earth environment. Without these past-life memories, the violence, competition, and greed would have shocked Phil's system. Dolores writes about Phil and his experiences as a Starperson in her brilliant book, *Keepers of the Garden* (Ozark Mountain Publishing).

Even though many Starpeople feel abandoned by their home planets, as if they were dropped off here on Earth without any say in the matter, they still retain connections to home. It's common for Starpeople to have ETs as their spirit guides. They also have etheric cords reaching to starships. And Starpeople frequently soul-travel to their home planets or starships during dreamtime or meditative sojourns.

Energy Work and Sensitivity

All of the Earth Angel realms report extreme sensitivity to energy from crowds, individuals, and places. Yet, the Starpeople realm is the most apt to study energy healing and make a career of it. In fact, it's amazing how many Starpeople make a living using their hands, whether through energy work or via tactile occupations such as landscaping, construction, hairstyling, manicuring, massage, and assembly-line labor.

Reiki seems to be the number one choice for energy healing work among Starpeople. This may be because Reiki energy originated from the Pleiades as a gift to Earth beings. It's interesting that Reiki energy clairvoyantly looks like thin bands of rainbow stripes, and this is also how the auras of Starpeople appear (which are visible in aura photos). They look like poles sticking vertically out of the Starperson's body, like hairs standing on end.

Starpeople are very attracted to symbols, codes, hieroglyphics, and sacred geometry, so it makes sense that they would adopt Reiki, since this healing method involves coded symbols that vibrate with different healing energies.

Toward the end of my Angel Therapy Practitioner certification courses, the students gather into groups corresponding to their respective Earth Angel realms. They then spend time together with other realm members, comparing notes about their similarities, and generally bonding with like-minded souls. I'll often interview the realm members to show patterns among them. During a recent course, every single person from the Starperson realm was also a Reiki master!

Starperson Terry says, "I am super-sensitive to energy. When I do Reiki, I can feel the shift of energy, and it pulls my hands where they should be for releasing the negative energies. Energy feels thick to me, like I'm pushing gum around."

And Starperson Nancy says, "When I do healing work, my hands heat up tremendously. I can feel the heat in a problem area on the person I'm working on."

Starpeople and Relationships

Starpeople may be born to non-Starpeople parents. These parents might not even be from any realm of the Earth Angels. As a result, the family cannot relate to the Starperson child, and the boy or girl ends up feeling disconnected from the birth family. Starperson Kathy recalls, "As a child, I constantly felt alone and different, even though I had five siblings."

Most planets don't have the birth and family systems of Earth life. Elsewhere, it's common for beings to be birthed in laboratories, à la "test-tube baby" processes. The emotional bonding that occurs in families here on Earth is alien to other planets as well. This is one reason why Starpeople may be perceived as friendly but distant. They're helpful, yet there's a certain degree of underlying coldness that's evident if someone attempts to create a close bond. You just never feel like you completely connect with a Starperson. And no wonder: Starpeople are task-oriented, not relationship-oriented. They have a job to do, and they aren't geared toward making relationships their top priority.

Starperson Scott says, "Realizing that I was a Starperson was a validation that has helped me to accept some of my colder traits, and the distance I sometimes feel toward others."

Starperson Terry has had a similar realization: "I'm different in a way that many don't understand. I feel like an outsider and very much of a loner. Most of the time, I'd rather be alone than with a group of people and their issues."

Being with other Starpeople is a way to feel accepted. Linda says, "My husband is a Starperson like me, and because of this, we connect 100 percent."

Linda's husband is 12 years younger than she is, and it seems that many female Starpeople have relationships with younger men. Typically, female Starpeople say, "I know that this man is from my home planet." Sometimes this age difference interferes with building a fully committed love relationship. It seems that male Starpeople may have come to Earth several years after the females.

When Starpeople do marry, they have very few children. Many Starpeople skip having children altogether. Linda says, "I'm 50 years old and have had a hysterectomy, so I won't be having any children. I always knew I wouldn't have kids—actually, I just didn't care either way. If my husband wanted some, fine. If he didn't, that was okay, too. But somehow I just *knew* I wouldn't bear children." Starperson Terry says that she's never been interested in what she calls "conventional family dynamics."

Starpeople often have C-section births. Perhaps that's because on other planets, vaginal-delivery births are unheard of, since babies are "bred" in laboratories. In fact, many planets' inhabitants are androgynous, without clear gender distinctions. Extraterrestrial babies aren't created through the Earthly methods of sexual intercourse, sperm, and eggs, but through a transfer of energies and the intention to create—a method portrayed in the movie *Cocoon*.

Starpeople may have a soul "contract" to *not* get married or have children while living an Earth life. They probably had no prior experiences with family and love relationships and didn't even think to put marriage and children into their Earth-life contract! Having a family may interfere with the Starperson's mission, and create karma that could keep him or her mired in Earth's reincarnation cycles.

Also, this may be the first lifetime that a Star-person has a clear-cut gender. The female may feel uncomfortable in her woman's body, and the male may feel like an awkward impostor posing as a man. Yet, when Starpeople get to Earth and see happy couples walking arm in arm, they may wish to share in that experience. Some Starpeople are able to manifest marriage and family, while others find that this type of union perpetually eludes them. If a Starperson does marry, it's usually later in life.

Handling Earth Life

As mentioned earlier, Starpeople are extra sensitive to violence. All of the Earth Angel realms report an aversion toward violence and conflict. However, of all the realms, Starpeople seem to be the most repulsed by fighting in any form. Linda says, "I can't tolerate violence in the least. I can't stand it when people even raise their voices. It's almost unbearable for me. It usually brings me to tears when someone scolds me." Most Starpeople surveyed told me that they don't watch, listen to, or read the news because it upsets them too much.

Starpeople see an eventual end to violence . . . if peace-loving men and women will take a stance in the form of prayer or guided action. In the meantime, Starpeople stay faithfully at their Earthly posts, being nice guys and gals in everyday situations. Yet, deep down, they're homesick for the peaceful life they once knew in a faraway place.

Starpeople who have learned how to handle Earth life say that it helps to connect with others in their realm. They're not difficult to spot if you look for their telltale physical characteristics. You can find Starpeople at electronics stores and conventions, at *Star Trek* conventions, at science-fiction film festivals, on scuba-diving boats, at Reiki and other energy-healing courses, in computer-science classes, and on message-board forums dedicated to these topics. Or, you can be sure to find them near the ocean. Every single Starperson surveyed said that living near water, especially the ocean, was a *must*. A high percentage of the scuba divers I've met are Starpeople, who escape from the everyday world by spending time underwater. After all, floating in water is similar to escaping gravity in outer space.

MaryKay explains this connection between Starpeople and water: "I realized that I need to live near a body of water to get balanced. I go there to feel the power of this huge body of water and the waves, and it's like a battery recharge for me."

Here are some other comments from Starpeople:

— **Starperson Linda says:** "My advice to other Starpeople is that it's okay to feel like you don't belong here on Earth . . . because you don't. Just be comfortable with this fact. You're special because you came here to assist this planet with accomplishing peace. You're on this planet by choice, to heal."

— **And Scott's advice for Starpeople is:** "Find others to connect with who share your common views, and keep smiling at all the insanity you're surrounded with. Teach tolerance and patience and especially love, because that's all there really is. And remember, this is only a temporary assignment!"

Life-Path Work for Starpeople

Starpeople are multitaskers and may not settle on one particular career as their life mission. They may, instead, dabble with several careers consecutively or simultaneously. Starpeople make wonderful Reiki masters, energy healers, massage therapists, chiropractors, and physical therapists. They also enjoy research, engineering, and support-staff work. However, the Starpeople must believe in the goals of the company they work for or they'll be miserable in their jobs. Starpeople are kind, hardworking, and efficient, yet often are perceived as being aloof or cold. They also prefer to be "under the radar." Therefore, they're better off doing solo work than being a spokesperson or a front-office employee.

Starpeople are the workaholics of the Earth Angel realms. They will work all day and night on any project that they believe in. Hybrid realms that carry the Starperson heritage, such as Incarnated Cherubs, Cosmic Angels, Galactic Knights, and Mystic Stars, also become workaholics.

It's important for Starpeople to learn how to balance work with self-care, relationships, relaxation, and fun. Starpeople have a sense of time urgency to get tasks done now, until they realize that the time system upon Earth calls for them to work progressively, not constantly.

Guidance and Suggestions If You're a Starperson

— Know that small acts of kindness do count. As a Starperson, you probably worry about Earth's future, or whether you're doing "enough." You'll feel better by remembering that the thousands of seemingly small acts of kindness you do add up to a huge contribution toward creating a peaceful planet.

— Seek out other Starpeople. It's essential to hang with like-minded folks. If you hold the intention of meeting other Starpeople, you'll soon easily attract them into your life. You can also meet Starpeople at conventions, classes, meetings, and on Internet message forums with extraterrestrial, energy healing, science fiction, scuba diving, or electronics themes.

— Appreciate your uniqueness. Your natural inclinations run counter to most Earthlings. Your standard of beauty is based more on what's on the inside than the outside—the opposite of many humans. Your priorities are more task oriented than relationship focused. So, Starperson, please honor your uniqueness, stand firm in your beliefs, and don't water down your capabilities by trying to conform.

— *Find balance.* There's more to life than working on your latest project. Part of your Earthly assignment is to open your heart chakra and experience love and emotions. Take time to develop relationships and enjoy fun leisure activities. Pursue a spiritual path that brings you joy and peace.

CHAPTER FOUR

THE WISE ONES:
REINCARNATED SORCERESSES, HIGH-PRIESTESSES, SORCERERS, WIZARDS, SHAMANS, AND WITCHES

You're likely a Wise One if you:

- Are wise beyond your years

- Feel a lot older than your chronological years

- Are fascinated with Earth-based spiritual paths such as shamanism, astrology, divination, and hermetics

- Are fond of the Arthurian, medieval, and Renaissance eras

- Wish that everyone would listen to your advice

- Prefer to dress in dark clothing and wear your hair longer (even if you have cut it short)

- Have a history of heart-related health concerns

- Have prematurely gray hair, wrinkles, or bags under your eyes

- Receive complaints from people that you talk "at them," instead of "with them"

- Dislike social small talk, and would prefer to teach or learn something important

- Know that you've been on Earth before, and that you carry the ancient wisdom with you

Intense. Exotic. Eccentric. The Wise Ones glow from the inside. They look like romance-novel characters, usually with long, silky hair; oval faces; and knowing eyes complete with a lifetime of shadows beneath them. Earth Angels from this realm possess profound wisdom and are highly intuitive. Their eyes are penetrating, and there's no point in pretending or lying to Wise Ones, because truth is apparent to them. Whimsical and flamboyant, Wise Ones love to dress in flowing garments reminiscent of romantic eras in the past. They may deliberately dress and act eccentrically, taking great pride in their personal style. There's a certain element of mystery accompanying each member of this realm. It's obvious, when first meeting the gaze of Wise Ones, that they *know*.

> When you look into the eyes of a Wise One, you see deep wisdom, knowingness, and often sorrow from witnessing the history of Earth and humanity. Wise Ones may also have well-earned bags or shadows beneath their eyes.

The Wise Ones are humans with past lives in which they learned how to channel their power into miraculous healings and manifestations, including the ability to affect the weather and material objects (through levitation, telekinesis, and the like). These are the extremely powerful and well-trained magicians of the human race who were called out of "retirement" from the spirit world in order to come back to Earth for the currently urgent situations on our planet.

Their energy is darker and heavier than the other Earth Angel realms. Wise Ones have a somber, serious, almost depressed energy, and they're sometimes quite stern. In relationships, they're highly opinionated in a helpful way. They're the "stage moms" and directors of their friends and family members, always knowing the best route for others to take. If someone wants solid advice, he or she should ask a Wise One.

Whereas the other realms are new to being human (or have past lives where they were Incarnated Angels, Elementals, and so on), the Wise Ones have been human for eons. Like the other Earth Angels, they feel "different." In fact, some Wise Ones proclaim, "I *am* different, and proud of it!" As one Incarnated Sorcerer put it: "In childhood, I realized I was different and didn't fit in, and that created difficulty—until I finally realized that my uniqueness was a benefit. I wasn't part of the masses or the norm; and when I matured, I realized that this was positive."

For that reason, the Wise Ones are more comfortable with Earth life than those in other realms. They're realistic, compassionate, and patient with people, and they've learned to enjoy their time here. Wise Ones aren't afraid to look at the shadow side of life like the other Earth Angel realms are. Incarnated Sorceress Linda spoke for many Wise Ones when she said, "I know I'm different from other people, but I don't really feel like an outsider because I basically don't care if most people like me or not." This detachment from other people's opinions is a hallmark of the Wise Ones.

The History of the Wise Ones

The common denominator of Wise Ones is the number of years they've logged learning to harness their magical powers. Some developed their own interest in metaphysics, and others were handpicked as children and schooled in the psychic arts. The Wise Ones have lived as High-Priestesses and Priests in Atlantis, ancient Greece, and Egypt; during Arthurian times; among the Mayans; as Essenes; and as native medicine men and women. They've witnessed civilizations destroyed, and people murdered for their spiritual beliefs. The Wise Ones know and appreciate the innate darkness within the human ego, but they have an even greater appreciation and respect for the heights to which humans are capable. And this is what they've come back to teach.

In heaven, many Wise Ones were comfortably enjoying the afterlife plane. They'd created paradise-like communities in the spirit world, complete with castles, gardens, and waterfalls. Everything seemed wonderful. But then the Wise Ones were approached by a committee of guides that was trying to enlist retired "spiritual soldiers" back into service. They asked the Wise Ones to return to Earth to teach and model peacefulness, and to remind people how to use their inner power and strength to create harmony.

Some Wise Ones reluctantly agreed to return to Earth. When they got here, they felt the heavy density of the shifting energy. A few Wise Ones, unable to handle this climate, exited immediately by willing their own deaths. Other Wise Ones relegated themselves to an Earth life, but felt depressed or angry about it.

The best-adjusted Wise Ones were those who resumed the study of Earth-based spirituality—such as astrology, Wicca, kabbalistic magic, hermetics, paganism, rituals, crystal healing, herbology, candle invocations, shamanism, and so forth.

Grethel says that one of the reasons why she believes she is a Reincarnated Sorceress is "because of my early interest in chants, herbs, magic wands, and the apparatus of ritual (candles, incense, water, and so on). I also had an 'imaginary friend' as a child who was a wizard. If that weren't enough, my great-aunt called me a 'sorceress' when I was young."

Members of the Wise Ones realm have spent lifetimes developing their spiritual and magical gifts. They're well practiced in the spiritual arts of manifestation, alchemy, and healing. They're born as psychic children who may view their gifts as being curses, especially if they're prescient about a forthcoming "negative" situation. The children may blame themselves for not diverting a tragedy, since they foresaw it. Yet, these psychic insights are often an opportunity for the individuals to pray about it. If they were supposed to intervene, they would have been clearly told what to do to prevent the situation.

The majority of Wise Ones whom I interviewed had vivid memories of past lives where they were witches, wizards, priests, and the like. Most of the Wise Ones surveyed had strong emotional reactions to the era of "witch burnings" from the years 1300 to

1700. Many of them have full or fragmented memories of being burned, hung, or otherwise killed for their spiritual differences. Sara, for example, says, "I have memories of being burned at the stake while people screamed and cursed at me. I remember being viciously tortured."

The "witch-burning craze" consisted of a mass superstition that anything bad—whether spoiled crops or sick children—was caused by a witch's spells. It was decided that the only way to purge this "evil" was through the burning of the witch's blood. Many of the witches were hunted by their neighbors, local governments, and churches. In more humane situations, they were killed before being tied to a pole and set on fire. Yet, in France, Germany, and Switzerland, most witches were burned alive.

Even those who weren't actually killed have conscious memories of this time period. They remember being afraid of the Inquisition, the Knights Templar, the Cathar trials (the Cathars were a pagan group in 13th-century Europe who were targeted by Pope Innocent III and were hunted and put to death), and the other various ways in which the witch hunts manifested. The threat of death hung over everyone during those times, and the memory makes Wise Ones nervous about fully reopening their spiritual gifts.

As a result, many Wise Ones hold back from unleashing their great power because of these ancient memories! Yet, the reason why they're here at this time is to teach and use those spiritual tools. A Wise One's purpose involves dusting off his or her psychic and spiritual healing abilities. And since we can only feel happy and fulfilled if we're engaged in our purpose, then it's necessary for Wise Ones to open and redevelop these gifts.

Since the Inquisition was persecution enacted jointly with the church and government, many Wise Ones are suspicious of organized religion. They loathe judgmental fundamentalists, and prefer to connect with the Creator outdoors rather than in a church or temple.

The Wise Ones have a special affinity with the Elemental kingdom, and vice versa. Not only do fairies and elves play a role in Earth-based spiritual practices, but deep friendships were forged between the Elementals and the Wise Ones. In ancient times, people recognized the benefits of working with the Elemental kingdom, yet the churches felt threatened by this power outside of their walls. So, a negative public-relations campaign against fairies, elves, and other Elementals was waged. To this day, many people are afraid of the beautiful Elementals.

Because the Elementals were so tied in with the Wise Ones in ancient and modern times, some Incarnated Elementals may believe that they're actually from the realm of the Wise Ones. That's due to the shared experiences and memories of these two realms. So, a female Incarnated Elemental may remember the witch burnings—not because she was burned, but because she witnessed this happening to her Wise One friends. She may be confused and think that these are *her* memories of being burned.

Yet, the differences between the two realms are clear: Wise Ones are more solemn, darker, and more serious than the playful, mischievous Incarnated Elementals. Wise Ones have long, oval faces and prefer to wear their hair long, too (even if they currently have it cut short for business reasons); while Incarnated Elementals have round faces, and often wear their hair short (except in the case of Incarnated Fairies and Mermaids). Male Wise Ones often wear their hair in ponytails or combed back with gel. Actors Della Reese, Angelica Huston, and Jimmy Smits are examples of the looks and intensity of this realm.

The Wise Ones may dress eccentrically or romantically, reflecting their favorite past-life period. Female Wise Ones prefer long dresses in dark colors, with chunky crystal necklaces, perhaps vintage or eco-friendly. Male Wise Ones favor woven shirts in natural fabrics or Renaissance-style shirts. The men may wear spiritually significant pendant necklaces, such as Celtic crosses or Ohm insignias. Wise Ones often love to attend Renaissance Fairs in full costume, where they can relive the highs and lows of their past lives.

The Wise Ones have dragons, wizards, and goddesses as spirit guides. They're very interested in the study of ancient eras that may be regarded as mythical, such as Avalon, Atlantis, and Lemuria. They collect wizard statues; and love books and movies dealing with magical themes, such as *The Lord of the Rings* series, the *Harry Potter* books, and anything related to Arthurian times. Many Wise Ones are also history buffs.

As Incarnated High-Priestess Marlies wrote: "I love Greek and Egyptian mythology. I can easily relate to Isis in the Egyptian tradition, and I love Pallas Athena—the goddess of wisdom and war. I deeply love her stories and her support she gave to Odysseus. With great passion, I studied ancient Greek, and I relate to all the goddesses of Olympus."

Wise Ones are also highly sensitive to moon phases—physically and emotionally affected by the full- and new-moon cycles. They often engage in "full-moon ceremonies" and celebrate the equinoxes.

Patterns among the Wise Ones

Interestingly, every Wise One surveyed knew their sun, moon, rising, and ascendant astrological signs. This was in sharp contrast to members surveyed from other realms, who often didn't even know their sun sign, and rarely knew their moon sign. Clearly, the Wise Ones are knowledgeable about astrology, and appreciative of its applications.

A high percentage of the Wise Ones surveyed had a past or current history of heart and cardiovascular health conditions. Mitral valve prolapse, high blood pressure, tachycardia, arrhythmia, heart murmurs, and heart attacks were rampant among this realm. Could this be from heartache within the realm, for loving Earth and her people so much, and watching its potential destruction? Or, is it residual pain from the witch hunts, where the Wise Ones' blood was burned and their hearts impaled with stakes?

Louise Hay says in *Heal Your Body* that the metaphysical meaning behind heart problems is "long-standing emotional problems." The Wise Ones have carried emotional pain for eons from their many Earthly lives—talk about long-standing! Other reasons for heart problems, according to Louise, include "lack of joy, hardening of the heart, and belief in strain and stress."

The Wise Ones whom I've met are intense individuals and hardworking teachers. They teach without ceasing, often by giving brief but deeply philosophical advice to people. Yet, the look in many Wise Ones' eyes reveals years of disappointment in their students. A Wise One recently told me, "If people would just take my advice, all of their problems would cease to be. I'm not being arrogant—I *just know* what would help them. Yet, most people ignore the advice and keep wallowing in their troubles." Since the Wise Ones' purpose is to teach and be way-showers, perhaps this frustration with their mission is their greatest heartbreak.

Like Elementals, Wise Ones aren't big fans of rules and regulations. However, Elementals invariably get caught when they break rules, whereas Wise Ones cast a cloak of invisibility over themselves. They rarely get caught breaking rules. When they do, Wise Ones may blame the Elementals for the infraction.

The Wise Ones in Relationships

Most Wise Ones long for a magical and mystical soul-mate marriage. They may feel the elusive presence of a kindred soul whom they've known for many lifetimes. This leads to a search for the beloved; and until he or she is found, the Wise One may choose to be romantically alone. Or worse, the Wise One may try settling for an unfulfilling relationship.

In previous lives, Wise Ones may have taken vows of chastity or celibacy. These unbroken vows can follow someone into a current life and wreak havoc. Wise One Audrey is a perfect example. She knew that she'd had past lives as a witch and also as a nun. As a past-lifetime witch, she was involved with pagan rituals, celebrating the earth, nature, and the human body. This often involved ceremonies with nudity and sexuality. The reigning powers at the time deemed this material focus to be heretical, and she was burned at the stake. In her next life, Audrey was a nun, where she took a vow of celibacy. Still, she retained her mystical interests and abilities.

In her present-day life, Audrey continued to practice spell castings, and knew how to manifest very well. However, her sex life was stunted in a sexless relationship with an impotent husband who was too proud to take medication or get sexual counseling. She finally "broke" her vows of celibacy, and was able to rekindle her sexuality. (You can break past-lifetime vows simply by saying aloud: "I ask that all vows that I made in prior lifetimes, which are not serving my Divine purpose in this lifetime, be now undone in all directions of time for everyone involved.")

So, Wise Ones do best in their love lives when they use their remarkable magical powers to manifest the love they seek. Even if their true beloved is not currently incarnate and is in the spirit world between-lives, Wise Ones can manifest wonderfully fulfilling love relationships with the power of their focused intentions.

Wise Ones do best when they have friends whom they respect and admire. Otherwise, the Wise One may have friends who are actually "clients." These "friendships" are one-sided, with the Wise One acting as teacher, and the friend acting as student. The Wise Ones never get a chance to discuss their own troubles because they're cast in the strong, empowered role.

Wise Ones are often accused of being know-it-alls. This accusation actually has a kernel of truth to it, because Wise Ones are tapped into the all-knowing collective unconscious. They're also highly psychic. Linda, a Reincarnated Sorceress, says, "Most often, I know what people are about to say. They get irritated with me because I finish their sentences."

The Wise Ones' children may accuse them of being controlling parents—again, because of this realm's compulsion to teach. Wise Ones can't *not* teach; however, they can soften their instruction so that it's more palatable. Instead of lecturing, for example, they can create a teaching experience that's entertaining and instructive.

As with their love lives, it's important for Wise Ones to use conscious visualizations of happy, healthy relationships with friends and family. They can use that remarkable power to see themselves surrounded by strong and loving friends who help *them*.

So if you think you're a Wise One, visualize and feel your children appreciating your teachings. Don't worry about how these manifestations will come about. Just know that they will. And then release the visions to the Universe so that they can manifest quickly and easily.

Wise Ones are frequently confronted by people of traditional religious faiths, who try to use fear or guilt to sway their beliefs. Wise Ones resist this form of religious marketing, because they have their own inner religion. Wise Ones may hold grudges against religion because of ancient memories of religious persecution in other lifetimes. Yet, Wise Ones can learn how to balance and release the past, so that they can develop a closeness with the Creator. Wise Ones develop their own personal blend of traditional and untraditional spirituality.

Magical Wise Ones

If you're a Wise One, you're a highly trained magician, and if some part of your life isn't working right now, take a proactive role in healing this area. If you passively wait for the Universe to direct you, you may find yourself spinning your wheels and going nowhere. That's because Wise Ones such as yourself are co-creators, and the Universe prefers to await your wishes and to fulfill them as asked. However, Wise Ones know from experience that not everything requested leads to happiness. For this reason, it's prudent to pray or ask for guidance *to know what to ask for.*

Faith in these abilities is crucial, even if it's just 5 or 10 percent faith. If you ask for something but harbor the fear that it might not happen, you'll block the manifestation. If you need to, you can "borrow" faith from one of your guides. Or, you can ask the Universe to clear away fears that are thwarting your full faith.

You may have, like many other Wise Ones, taken vows in your past lives as a spiritual aspirant or devotee (such as a nun or a monk). Among the most common are vows of suffering, self-sacrifice or retribution, poverty, chastity, virginity, celibacy, obedience, and silence. Unless these vows are severed, they can follow you to Earth and place barriers in your love and sexual areas, finances, and life in general. No one is truly free until these past-life vows are broken. The only healthy vows are those that *you* decide upon—the ones you make with yourself. Even then, you'll want to regularly review them to see if they're still valid.

Break these vows and their effects by strongly affirming:

"I hereby sever any vows of suffering, self-sacrifice, or retribution that I may have made, in all directions of time. I rescind any negative effects of these vows, now and forever."

Then, repeat this phrase for other vows (poverty, celibacy, and so on). Since these vows often involved signing a document with your own blood, you'll need to break the vow with an even greater amount of power. It's especially powerful to light a candle (which helps release negativity and break up stagnant situations) and conduct the ceremony during a full moon, which is the time of release. Then, stand up and stamp your foot down strongly as you make each statement aloud. Really say it like you mean it when you sever those vows!

Wise Ones, always remember the power of the word. Become clear about what you desire, and then command—through words—that it happen. You are a master spell caster, both in the name of your fears *and* your heart's desires. So, you just as easily create self-fulfilling prophecies in the direction of your ego's fear-based dictates as well as your higher self's loving visions. Command your ego to silence, and direct your higher self to increase the volume of its voice.

As your manifestations appear in tangible form, welcome them with open arms. Wise Ones sometimes push away manifestations for fear that they don't deserve them. Remember, though, that these manifestations are tools that help your teaching and healing practice. Your students and clients deserve to be helped by a Wise One whose material needs are met. Put all scarcity or vows of suffering behind you now, Wise One.

Life-Path Work for Wise Ones

As a Wise One, you're a natural-born leader who's respected because of your charisma, your air of confidence, the way that you carry yourself, and your personal power. People naturally respect and admire you; they're even intimidated by you. So, they feel comfortable following your lead.

Because of your many lifetimes of spiritual learning and teaching, you'd probably enjoy a career as a spiritual teacher, astrologer, psychic, healer, channeler, or oracle-card reader. Most Wise Ones don't do well as employees or followers, unless you respect your boss or leader. You would make an excellent company president or entrepreneur, especially with your organizational skills combined with your intuitive knowledge of how to improve situations.

However, you, like most Wise Ones, would feel frustrated working with unmotivated audiences or clients who won't take your advice.

Hybrids of Wise Ones

As you'll read in Part II, there are variations of Wise Ones blended with other realms. They include the Knights Paladin, Mystic Angels, Mystic Stars, and Mystic Mers.

Guidance and Suggestions If You're a Wise One

— *Honor the power of the word.* Use vigilance with your thoughts and words to ensure that they mirror what you want, not what you fear. You manifest so quickly that you can't afford to think or talk about your fears. Focus all your energies on manifesting your desires and life purpose.

— *Honor your past.* Engage in past-life regressions to clear away leftover emotions that could be holding you back today. Read books and watch movies related to your past lives.

— *Be aware of the power of your temper.* When a Wise One slings anger toward another person, it's akin to casting a dark spell. Use your power carefully; and think twice before cursing someone, as this can hurt other people as well as come back to haunt you.

— *Teach what's important to you.* You're always teaching by example. One reason to pull yourself up to your highest level is to inspire others. You elected to come to Earth to teach about human potential, so it's important for you to model that in your own life.

— *Laugh and play.* Even though you have a vital mission, it's important to inject regular doses of playfulness into your life. Sincerity, not seriousness, is called for in your mission. Laughter also helps you heal any heartbreak suffered in this life or past ones.

— *Gain respect, not intimidation.* Wielding your power so that other people are afraid of you isn't soul-satisfying. It's lonely to be feared by others! But using your power to gain respect is deeply fulfilling.

PART II

BLENDED REALMS AND HYBRIDS

During my certification programs, I explain the various realms in detail. I then ask audience members to meet with members of their realm. Those who are unsure of their realm are encouraged to join each group to discover which one feels the most comfortable. People can instantly sense if they belong in a group.

Some audience members have felt that they belonged in two of the realm groups. For example, several said that they couldn't decide whether they fit better into the Incarnated Angel or the Wise One categories. I thought that they must be souls who were evolving from one realm into another, so I'd send them to the Evolvers, Shape-shifters, or Dabblers group.

I soon realized that these folks were from realms other than the four core ones (Incarnated Angel, Incarnated Elemental, Starperson, and Wise One). I surveyed and had conversations with students, and we discovered new realms together. In fact, we are *still* in the process of uncovering new realms!

The following chapters describe the realms that we are presently aware of. If you feel you belong in more than one—or don't fit into any—it could be that you are a member of a realm that still needs to be revealed and studied. You could be the trailblazer who awakens all of us to an awareness of your realm!

CHAPTER FIVE

MYSTIC ANGELS

You're probably a Mystic Angel if you:

- Only apologize to move things along

- Feel a connection to Archangel Raphael, the healing angel

- Acknowledge the shadow side of life

- Currently have, or in the past have had, addictions

- Consider yourself tougher and stronger than the average person

- Are prone to cussing and colorful language

- Dress with an edge, such a Gothic look, with tattoos or piercings

- Are interested in esoteric spirituality, such as astrology and traditional tarot

Mystic Angels are half Wise Ones and half Incarnated Angels. Mystic Angels share many characteristics with Incarnated Angels, in that they're helpful and caring. Yet, since they've had several lifetimes on Earth (as Incarnated Angels), they're also street-smart and edgy. They might cuss, abuse alcohol, smoke, or gamble . . . yet they're still angels.

> When you look into the eyes of a Mystic Angel, you see compassion.

Mystic Angels appreciate rules because they abhor chaos. Like Incarnated Angels, they'll apologize—yet they only say "I'm sorry" because it's a fast way to clear up conflict, not because they feel guilty.

Mystic Angels have the hard-won wisdom that comes from many lifetimes of helping in the trenches of wars and conflict. Even though they've seen it all,

Mystic Angels still retain some faith in the goodness of humanity.

Mystic Angels aren't afraid to acknowledge the shadow side of life. They clearly see the ego issues behind human dramas. The focus and language of a Mystic Angel are a bit darker and earthier than those of an Incarnated Angel (which is a realm that doesn't like to look at or acknowledge problems or shadows).

Because Mystic Angels acknowledge the ego, they are also compassionate about people falling into ego-traps. They understand how it feels to be afraid, angry, and frustrated. While an Incarnated Angel may not understand why someone is angry, or may be afraid of anger, the Mystic Angel sees this emotion as a normal part of the human experience. A pure Wise One would likely lecture or scold someone for being in their ego. But a Mystic Angel would say, "Yes, I understand, because I've been there, too."

One Mystic Angel described her realm's characteristics in this way: "We're healers who are know-it-alls. Because we've been killed in previous lifetimes, we're often afraid to come out of the spiritual closet. But when we do, we fly high and fast in putting our purpose into action."

Life Purpose and Career

Mystic Angels aren't timid in front of audiences, as Incarnated Angels are. With their Wise One heritage, Mystic Angels make wonderful teachers, speakers, and workshop presenters. They love to teach about healing techniques and offer tips for happy living.

Past-life memories (conscious or unconscious) of being killed due to their spiritual healing and teaching work can keep them locked in fears, however. The best way to release these fears is by having a past-life regression with a qualified therapist (usually a highly experienced hypnotherapist). A past-life regression, coupled with calling upon Archangel Raziel ("the angel of God's secrets"), can help Mystic Angels move past these fears. When they do, Mystic Angels greatly enjoy writing and teaching.

Mystic Angels who ignore their spiritual path become depressed and anxious. For this realm, spirituality is an absolute necessity! Just about anything that helps the Mystic Angel to feel connected to heaven—reading spiritual books, taking metaphysical classes, receiving energy healing sessions, meditating and praying, going on nature walks, doing artwork or yoga—is necessary for maintaining health and happiness.

In Relationships

Mystic Angels are leather-and-lace, tough-and-gentle. So, a Mystic Angel needs a lot of cuddling, tenderness, respect, and an appreciative audience. Being half Wise One means that Mystic Angels do have all the answers . . . provided that their loved ones are open to hearing about it. Frequently, Mystic Angels are taunted for being know-it-alls. Yet, because they are half Incarnated Angel, they are also very emotional.

So in relationships, Mystic Angels need to reveal their emotions and be a bit vulnerable. Otherwise, people will just react to the tough outer shell. A Mystic Angel needs tender moments, and this will only happen if she has the courage to show the sweet side of herself to others.

Mystic Angels are also prone to an imbalance of giving and receiving. It's easy for Mystic Angels to assume to role of caretaker and teacher, and then to resent that their needs aren't being met. A Mystic Angel needs to teach her loved ones that she is a human, too. Although she's extremely strong and wise, she also needs to receive. This calls for the Mystic Angel to practice asking for—and accepting—help from others.

When she learns to receive, the Mystic Angel begins to manifest and heal at a whole new, high level!

CHAPTER SIX

KNIGHTS PALADIN AND GALACTIC KNIGHTS

You're likely a Knight Paladin or Galactic Knight if you:

- Are the protector of your loved ones
- Are good at guarding secrets
- Are reliable and keep your promises
- Believe in justice
- Have excellent posture

- Feel a strong connection to Archangel Michael
- Are fascinated by movies and books about knights
- Are strong, emotionally and physically
- Wish that everyone would behave with integrity

This realm was uncovered by my son Grant. As you may recall, Grant was the person who originally pointed out the Wise One realm to me. After we delineated this realm, Grant saw that he actually fit into a subcategory of Wise Ones that we initially called "Knights." However, that term wasn't accurate because it implied pure warriors. So the term *Paladin* was suggested by two members of this realm. Paladin, pronounced *pal-AH-den,* refers to a magical or holy knight who crusades in the name of upholding goodness and order. Historical Paladins were wizards who cast spells to complete their missions.

Knights Paladin share many qualities with Mystic Angels in that they're half Wise One and half angel. Mystic Angels express their angelic side through healing others, either with their teaching wisdom or with their energy. Knights Paladin represent the protective-guardian side of angels. Mystic Angels express Archangel Raphael's healing energy, while Knights Paladin express Archangel Michael's sword-wielding energy.

Knights Paladin are the custodians of orderliness; and the upholders of truth, sacred secrets, and civility. They are completely trustworthy, able to keep secrets (unless leaking the secret would help uphold justice), and extremely helpful to loved ones and strangers. Knights Paladin feel uncomfortable in social settings, unless they're discussing a topic of personal interest. They're chivalrous and polite, yet they can also be staunch and unyielding when their values are threatened. Knights Paladin refuse to compromise when it comes to ethics. Remember that Incarnated Angels (which Knights Paladin are blended from) respect authority, organization, and rules, especially when they believe in those rules.

In prior lifetimes, members of this realm served as Knights Templar; members of the Round Table; the Twelve Noble Peers of the *chansons de geste* of medieval legend; and bodyguards of high-priests, high-priestesses, saints, and sages. Knights Paladin tend to have large bodies and muscular strength. They stand tall with egoless pride; and their alert eyes notice everything.

Knights Paladin have a lifelong fascination with knights, suits of armor, stories of the Round Table, castles, and jousting. They love video games, books, and movies involving wartime strategies, sword fights, and redemption. Famous Knights Paladin include Joan of Arc, King Arthur, King David, and Sir Lancelot.

> The eyes of a Knight Paladin are intense, clear, and focused, like a bodyguard on high alert.

Knights Paladin also have Eastern counterparts in samurai and Shaolin monks, who incorporate breath work, posture, self-discipline, and wisdom in their approaches to managing life.

Knights Paladin make wonderful advocates and activists who champion the causes they believe in. They do well in areas of law, politics, writing, speaking, coaching, campaigning, and leading. Knights Paladin who are Indigos (the generation of highly sensitive natural-born leaders and visionaries) can make intense and inspirational leaders.

Galactic Knights

Knights Paladin are protectors of Earth and her inhabitants, and Galactic Knights are protectors of Earth's relationship to other planets. They are the enforcers of universal order among humans, to ensure that our home planet stays intact.

Galactic Knights are a three-way blend of Wise One, Incarnated Angel, and Starperson. They are the Jedi Knights of the solar system who have an important mission of protection.

Galactic Knights work with Archangel Michael and the universal energies. They follow their inner guidance without question (unless their ego-based insecurities and/or addictions interfere). Like Knights Paladin, the Galactic Knights have a charismatic power and body posture that takes charge of troubling situations. They are natural leaders who manage others with wisdom and loving firmness.

Galactic Knights are fascinated with outer space, science fiction, and ETs. They also love superhero movies and may engage in "cosplay," dressing in costume as their favorite superhero. Galactic Knights know that good-versus-evil is a very real drama in our physical world, and they are determined to help good to win!

Life Purpose and Career

Many Knights Paladin are drawn to the armed services, jobs in security, and police work, which are modern equivalents of knight orders. They also study or join secret societies, such as the Freemasons, Knights Templar, and Rosicrucians. Yet, modern-day Knights Paladin often must take solo missions to fulfill their destinies. Instead of following the king's orders, today's Knights Paladin must follow the orders of their internal guidance. Joining the military or police force may hamper their freedom to follow this inner wisdom, or could even dampen the voice of their intuition itself.

Regardless of profession, every Knight needs to follow a spiritual path of engaging in protective pursuits for the sake of loved ones and the planet. This could involve visualizing a protective energy shield around Earth, praying for protection, or another spiritual protection method that is received through Divine guidance.

In Relationships

Knights make wonderfully loyal and trustworthy partners. You can always rely on them to be punctual, protective, and honest (although they may withhold information to protect their loved ones). They want the best for their loved ones, and will sacrifice their own comfort and safety to help family and friends.

Often, though, Knights are perceived as overly protective or even smothering. The Knights are so focused on shielding their loved ones that they may seem to stomp on the other person's freewill choices. The Knight has admirable intentions of being protective, but the loved one feels controlled. Fortunately, Knights are reasonable and can negotiate ways of looking out for their loved ones while giving them some space.

Galactic Knights have the Starperson characteristic of being task-oriented workaholics, instead of relationship-oriented. This may frustrate family or friends who wish to discuss their feelings. A Galactic Knight would be smart to acquire an "emotions vocabulary" so that he can use feeling-based words (such as *happy, frustrated, excited, peaceful,* and so on) in conversations with non-Starperson loved ones.

CHAPTER SEVEN

ALADDIN GENIES

You may be an Aladdin Genie if you:

- Believe in magic and have had many magical experiences

- Love the warmth and beauty of the desert and mountains

- Are an entertaining storyteller

- Love music and dancing

- Prefer spicy food

- Love bright and warm colors like red, orange, and yellow

- Live for the sunshine

- Are good at granting wishes that make others happy

Our next hybrid realm is a blend of the Wise One, Incarnated Angel, and Incarnated Elemental realms, resulting in the Aladdin Genies. The men and women of this magical realm are entertaining, sweet, and delightfully unpredictable. In a way, you could say that Aladdin Genies are the fairies of the desert and the fire element.

Aladdin Genies are all about fiery passion, so they have an extra zest for life that others find irresistible, charming, and inspiring. Aladdin Genies throw their whole soul and energy into whatever project they're involved in.

Aladdin Genies are magical wish-granters, who will bend the physical laws of heaven and earth to make their loved ones happy. They know how to manifest like true magicians, and their wishes come true rapidly. For this reason, Aladdin Genies especially need to guard their thoughts so that they don't manifest their fears into reality!

> The eyes of an Aladdin Genie twinkle with magic and a faraway look into the future possibilities for us all.

Aladdin Genies are Bedouin-like nomads who move a lot, as they feel guided to experience adventure and bring joy and entertainment to the next town. They love and welcome the new!

Since Aladdin Genies are drawn to the element of fire, it's not surprising that they prefer to live near or in the desert or dry mountain areas. They can't withstand cold weather, but because of their hardy strength, they will endure the cold temporarily.

Perhaps this is why Aladdin Genies love spicy food so much, as it keeps them warm on chilly nights! In fact, they like anything that reminds them of warmth and sunshine—such as bold, vibrant reds, oranges, and yellows; sparkly crystals and gemstones; and the sun's rays on a summer day. Aladdin Genies love the beach because of the sand, but don't ask them to go swimming in the water! It's too cold and wet for their taste. Aladdin Genies prefer to wear light and airy clothing, which may even be revealing, since they do have a fiery and passionate sensual side.

Aladdin Genies share the Incarnated Elemental's love for music and dancing, as a route to elevating their energy and connecting to higher realms. Plus, there's the added bonus of entertaining others (a primary objective of Aladdin Genies).

They are master manifesters who understand the science of the Law of Attraction and other universal energy laws. They believe in magic and apply it to benefit their lives and those of others.

Life Purpose and Career

Aladdin Genies have the Wise One ability to see others' potential and to know the answers and best steps to take. They make wonderful counselors, psychics, psychologists, spiritual advisors, and life coaches.

Think of desert nomads sitting around a campfire, telling stories, and you'll get an insight into the Aladdin Genies' tremendous talent for storytelling. They make wonderfully entertaining teachers, writers, actors, singers, musicians, dancers, speakers, and preachers. Aladdin Genies are very comfortable with the spotlight and enjoy being the center of attention.

After eons of sitting beneath the starry skies of the deserts, Aladdin Genies have a fascination with astrology and astronomy, and they excel in occupations related to the stars and planets.

In Relationships

Wish-granting is the greatest joy for Aladdin Genies, and they love helping other people's dreams come true. However, this can easily come at personal expense to the human Aladdin Genie. Like the Incarnated Angels, from which Aladdin Genies stem, it's essential that they balance giving and receiving.

If the Aladdin Genies focus only on making others happy, then they're giving away their personal power to those other people. The unbalanced Aladdin Genie feels unhappy if he or she has been unable to please everyone. The balanced Aladdin Genie wishes everyone would be happy, but realistically acknowledges other people's freewill choices . . . which may not include happiness.

ATLANTEANS

You're probably an Atlantean if you:

- Are fascinated by pyramids and sacred geometry
- Have a stronger-than-normal fondness for dolphins
- Feel that you lived during Atlantean times
- Have a phobia about drowning
- Have wonderful posture
- Love crystals
- Have long dark hair

- Relate more to ascended masters than to angels

- Love Grecian, Egyptian, Mayan, and Incan cultures and spiritual paths

- Are deeply concerned about government and corporate corruption

The Atlanteans are people who lived and perished during the time of Atlantis. They have returned to Earth to impart their knowledge and wisdom to the human race, to prevent a recurrence of the tragic end of Atlantis. That civilization sank when a few corrupt government leaders decided to use the power of sunlight directed through crystals like a laser, to overtake other landmasses. Unfortunately, their weapons backfired and sent their own continent to the bottom of the sea.

As a result, Atlanteans today have phobias of drowning in the ocean. They enjoy being near the sea, but they don't trust it. However, the Atlantean who overcomes this phobia becomes an excellent swimmer. Atlanteans share a deep bond with dolphins, who were also inhabitants of their utopian society.

Atlanteans are a blend of Wise One, Incarnated Angel, and Starperson. They possess the wisdom and confidence of a Wise One, the loving and giving heart of an Incarnated Angel, and the technical nature of a Starperson.

Atlanteans are easily recognizable by their posture and other distinguishing physical characteristics. They stand and walk perfectly erect, as if they are balancing a book on their head. Their hair is usually dark, long, and silky, and their eyes are brown. Atlanteans may have a dark complexion as well. They prefer to dress in Grecian style of clothing and jewelry, and they are fascinated by Greek and Egyptian spirituality and culture.

Because of their particular spiritual principles, Atlanteans relate more to ascended masters (such as Jesus, Buddha, Isis, and Quan Yin) than to angels. In fact, many of the original Atlanteans who survived the deluge arrived on the shores of Mexico, Peru, Egypt, and Greece and began teaching their wisdom. The cultures appreciated the high-level teachings so much that they elevated the Atlantean teachers to demigod status. Some of these teachers include Pallas Athena in Greece, Hermes Trismegistus in Egypt and Greece, and Quetzalcoatl in Aztec and Toltec Mexico (for more information, please read *Archangels & Ascended Masters*).

Atlanteans also possess an innate respect for pyramids and other forms of sacred geometry. This makes sense, considering that Atlantis was a pyramid-building society. After their demise, those who survived began building pyramids in their new locations, such as the Yucatán; Peru; and Egypt.

> The eyes of an Atlantean are wise, knowing, and filled with faith in the magic of tapping into the Universe's gifts.

Life Purpose and Career

Atlantis was a highly evolved society, as Plato himself described in his book *Timaeus and Critias*. They used the power of free solar energy for aerial transportation, healing, and daily living. Atlanteans living today are obsessed with ridding the world of dependency on nuclear power and fossil fuels. They urgently desire to recapture the power of the sun, tide, and wind to freely fuel human needs. Of course, those who make money on the nonrenewable forms of power are threatened by free power. So the Atlanteans find themselves in the same power struggle with corrupt government and corporate leaders as they did in their previous time in Atlantis. Therefore, Atlanteans make powerful examples of integrity when they work for charities and other groups determined to save the environment.

Atlanteans possess the free-energy knowledge from their Starperson heritage, so they are also highly interested in anything related to sci-fi, energy healing, engineering, and inventions. They also make wonderful teachers, healers, and writers about the esoteric arts of dream interpretation, sacred geometry, and past-life regression.

Their close relationships with dolphins and the ocean make Atlanteans wonderful advocates for protecting the sea and her inhabitants. Audiences naturally follow the leadership qualities of Atlanteans who, with their stately posture and commanding style, become successful speakers and teachers.

In Relationships

Atlanteans are task-oriented, due to their Starperson heritage. They may become workaholics who are too busy for a relationship. The Atlantean mind is always busy, and they've developed the ability to be skilled multitaskers. So, with a little reminder from a loved one, Atlanteans are eager to please others and will make room in their schedules for relationships. After all, they are part Incarnated Angel.

CHAPTER NINE

INCARNATED CHERUBS

You're most likely an Incarnated Cherub if you:

- Are highly romantic
- Decorate your home with Victorian charm, such as lace, pearls, and candles
- Have long, healthy hair (usually brown or black) that you take the time to style
- Fall in love easily
- Are good at matchmaking
- Have a small mouth with pouty lips
- Love to dress up and/or wear makeup

- Have eyebrows that are plucked and groomed
- Don't like to get messy
- Adore romantic books, movies, and television shows
- Are frequently told that you're "cute"
- Love to go shopping and have no trouble spending money on yourself
- Generously treat your loved ones to gifts and fun activities
- Dream of having a perfectly romantic partner
- Adore going to the spa and getting massages, facials, and other treatments

Statues and paintings of cherub angels date back to ancient times. The Bible refers to *cherubim,* as the plural of cherub angels who occupy a high level of the angelic realms. The most famous cherub is Cupid, who represents this realm's focus on love and relationships, particularly of the romantic variety.

Incarnated Cherubs are cherub angels who have taken on human form to fulfill God's will of love on this planet. Cherubs are one-half Incarnated Angel and one-half Starperson. From their Incarnated Angel heritage, Cherubs have loving hearts filled with joy that they wish to share with everyone. Both Cherubs and Incarnated Angels are obsessed with making everyone around them happy. But the big distinction is that Cherubs also love to make *themselves* happy, while Incarnated Angels ignore their own needs and only focus on others.

> When you look into the eyes of a Cherub, you see beauty, love, and a childlike awe of life (and usually lots of eye makeup and long eyelashes).

Incarnated Cherubs are usually petite and carry a bit of extra weight, but are generally thinner than their Incarnated Angel counterparts. That's because Cherubs love to indulge in healthy self-care such as fitness routines.

Cherubs have childlike heart-shaped faces, usually framed by cascading hair that they set into waves or curls (females) and long hair for males. Their hair is often dark brown or black. They take pride in their hair and in dressing well, and are considered "cute."

I call Incarnated Cherubs the "spa angels," because they adore getting massages, facials, manicures, pedicures, and the latest beauty treatment. Their bathroom counters are filled with skin potions, makeup, and bottles of cologne. They love to shop and have a taste for the most luxurious clothes and opulent home decor. Cherubs love all forms of beauty, especially when it evokes a romantic feeling. They love pearls, velvet, marble, tapestries, and gilded, carved wooden furniture. Everything is first-class and five-star for the Cherub realm!

Cherubs are also very generous; they love to treat their friends to shopping sprees and spa dates, even when they really can't afford to do so. Cherubs are generous like their Incarnated Angel heritage, but the big difference is that Cherubs have no trouble receiving and giving to themselves.

The Starperson influence can be seen in some physical aspects that both realms share. Cherubs and Starpeople have small mouths and large eyes. Cherubs accentuate these two features with lipstick and eye makeup, whereas Starpeople eschew any type of makeup. Cherubs also have much fuller lips than Starpeople, with the classic pouty bow-shaped mouth that you see in Victorian cherub angel paintings.

Female Cherubs and Starpeople also pluck their eyebrows into thin lines. Cherubs obsess over their facial perfection, pouring their workaholism into the pursuit of perfectly plucked eyebrows and a flawless complexion.

Cherubs adore the beauty of living near the ocean, but won't actually go into the water because they don't like to mess up their hair, ruin their manicure, or sun-damage their skin. Cherubs work hard to keep themselves coiffed and fancy.

Life Purpose and Career

Cherubs are obsessed with romantic love, and they excel in careers involving matchmaking, writing romance novels, and marriage counseling.

They also have a penchant for beauty; they do very well in interior decorating (especially for luxury homes), fashion design, working as a professional personal shopper or stylist, cosmetology, feng shui, and the arts. In addition, the Cherub's appreciation for spas means that they would enjoy working in this industry (provided they are treated regularly to massages themselves).

Cherubs are workaholics, but they also dream of a life of riches and luxury, where they don't need a job. They'd rather stay home, go to the mall, or get treatments at the spa.

In Relationships

Cherubs and Starpeople are both task-oriented rather than relationship-oriented. While the romance-obsessed Cherub may seem to be a people person, she actually has a tendency to view others through the lens of a romantic fantasy rather than seeing the real person. Cherubs put their partners on idealized pedestals, wanting them to behave like romance-novel heroes and heroines. Then when the human characteristics are revealed, the Cherub loses interest.

Cherubs love the feeling of falling in love, and they develop romantic crushes very easily and quickly. Therefore, Cherubs are prone to "love addictions," where they get hooked on the high of romantic love. It's then that other people are viewed as vehicles to get the romantic-love high. Being aware of this tendency is a first step. Getting counseling from a qualified therapist who can help the Cherub regain the connection with Divine love is a good second step. There are also online and in-person Sex and Love Addicts Anonymous 12-step groups that can help Cherubs find real romantic relationships, instead of fantasy romance.

Cherubs tend to be "serial monogamists" who go from one relationship to another. A Cherub who takes the time to get to know the real person before quickly entering into a love relationship enjoys a longer-term and more satisfying partnership.

If compulsive shopping becomes an economic hardship for the Cherub, there is also help available by calling upon the Angels of Abundance (a group of cherubic spiritual angels who guide and support our material needs), and also working with a qualified counselor or with Shopaholics Anonymous 12-step groups.

Mystic Stars and Cosmic Angels

You're probably a Mystic Star or Cosmic Angel if you:

- Believe that angels have extraterrestrial origins

- Are extremely open-minded

- Have a thin body and straight hair

- Feel socially awkward, even though you deeply care for people's welfare

- Pray for world peace regularly
- Feel a connection to other planets or star systems
- Engage in unique forms of energy-healing work

As you've seen, there are countless combinations of the four core realms of Incarnated Angel, Incarnated Elemental, Wise One, and Starperson. Each combination creates a unique persona and different life-purpose focus.

Mystic Stars are a blend of Starpeople and Wise Ones. Natural-born teachers, they bring universal knowledge to Earth. Their teachings have the global purpose of inspiring peace, by giving humans helpful information to reduce their stress levels.

Mystic Stars are generally thin and lanky people with long, straight hair and large eyes. They have a facial expression of constant wonder, as they love discovering, learning, and teaching about new insights. They are the galactic explorers of the Earth Angel realms.

Mystic Stars have very exotic, different-looking eyes that reflect their serious, somber, and intense passion for teaching. Females may have the Starperson penchant for plucking or tattooing their eyebrows thinly or unusually.

Life Purpose and Career

Mystic Stars are happiest when they're both learning *and* teaching. Easily bored and distracted, they need constant new challenges to keep their minds occupied. Mystic Stars are thrilled to learn about any topic, and they have curious minds that want to find out all of the details. After they absorb all there is to know about a topic, they begin to teach others. This receiving-and-giving process can be very balanced and keep the Mystic Star satisfied for a lifetime.

Mystic Stars can do well at anything they focus on. They are highly intelligent, hardworking, dedicated, and reliable. Other people enjoy being with Mystic Stars, even if they don't quite understand the super-genius Mystic Star mind-set.

For the highest level of business success, Mystic Stars should learn and apply all that they can of human etiquette and social decorum. Overcoming the social awkwardness of their Starperson heritage will help Mystic Stars go far in the business world.

In Relationships

Mystic Stars are highly sensitive and can feel the energy of other people's emotions. They often become uncomfortable around others, and can sometimes act socially awkward. Mystic Stars combat social stress by teaching facts and philosophies, instead of engaging in small talk.

Mystic Stars unwittingly try to teach family members, whose eyes glaze over from an overload of technical information. So, Mystic Stars do best when they pay attention to cues from their students and audience members, and watch for waning attention levels. Mystic Stars are so intelligent that they may unwittingly talk over someone's head. Without dumbing down their lessons, Mystic Stars can tailor their teachings so that they're more easily digestible.

In both their personal and professional lives, Mystic Stars will encounter satisfaction by taking the time to study and apply information about how to achieve success in relationships. Mystic Stars should read lots of books and attend seminars about relationships and interpersonal communication skills.

Cosmic Angels

Another hybrid is the Cosmic Angel, who is one-half Starperson and one-half Incarnated Angel. You might think of Cosmic Angels as being the high-vibrational guardian angels of the Universe. They are the angels who protect the "big picture" of all the beings on all of the planets. This is a big job! Fortunately, Cosmic Angels are up for the task, as they carry the Starperson workaholic trait.

Cosmic Angels are usually thin, like most Star-people. They are often tall and don't spend much time on makeup, self-care, or style of dress (although they may pluck their eyebrows thin, which is a Starperson trait). They are task-oriented and entirely focused on completing the job of healing people, and ultimately healing the planet.

> Cosmic Angels have a faraway knowingness, an ungrounded look, and helpful concern in their eyes.

Life Purpose and Career

Perhaps more than the other Earth Angel realms, the Cosmic Angel must hold a meaningful career in order to feel happy. Cosmic Angels will throw all of their time and energy into any field for which they feel passion. They excel at being administrators for charities and other companies that are helping the planet.

Cosmic Angels would be frustrated in any job where they can only help a small number of people. They feel a sense of urgency in helping everyone, everywhere simultaneously. They would enjoy doing spiritual teaching on a massive scale, such as blogging on the Internet, or leading spiritual teleclasses with many participants. Fortunately, the Cosmic Angel can overcome the Starperson shyness by focusing on the bigger picture of being a leader for the greater good of all.

In Relationships

Because of her Angel-Starperson blend, the Cosmic Angel may have internal battles that negatively impact her relationships. On the one hand, her Incarnated Angel heritage is cuddly, loving, and emotional. But then her Starperson side is a workaholic who finds emotions and relationships to be distracting and unnecessary.

So the Cosmic Angel would do well to find a balance between work and social life. For example, dedicate certain hours to work and others to relationship development. Once the Cosmic Angel realizes that peace on Earth begins at home, she will gladly agree to turn off her computer and have some one-on-one time with her loved ones.

LEPRECHAUNS

You're probably a Leprechaun if you:

- Can easily make other people laugh

- Love to have an appreciative audience

- Think practical jokes are fun and funny

- Use humor while teaching others

- Have a Celtic heritage or appearance

- Are unusually lucky, and bring luck to others

- Are criticized for being immature

- Are in a serious mood sometimes and a silly mood at other times

When we think of Leprechauns, little men in green suits come to mind. However, the Earth Angel realm of Leprechauns includes a wide variety of body shapes, sizes, and clothing styles. There are both male and female Leprechauns, and many members of this realm *do* look like giant Leprechauns. Yet, it's what's on the inside rather than outside that distinguishes this realm from the others.

Leprechauns are half Wise Ones and half Incarnated Elementals. They have the wisdom that comes from many lifetimes lived; a down-to-earth, commonsense approach to life; a deep connection to nature; and a wicked sense of humor.

> One minute when you look into a Leprechaun's eyes, you see the serious intensity of a wise teacher. The next minute, though, you'll see the mischievous look of a seven-year-old who's about to play a prank.

To understand the Leprechaun realm, let's look at their history. One of the original peoples of Ireland were called the Tuatha Dé Danann, which means the "children of Dana" or the "people of Dana." Dana was a Celtic creator goddess. The Tuathas possessed magical abilities to shape-shift and time-travel and were considered demigods in some circles. They fought battles to maintain possession of Ireland, but eventually were defeated by the invading Gaels. Instead of leaving their island, though, the Tuathas shape-shifted into another dimension and became Leprechauns. Today, they still run Ireland, yet are only visible to those with open minds and hearts.

Earth Angels from the Leprechaun realm are half Wise One and half Elemental. They possess ancient knowledge about magic, healing, and manifestation, like Wise Ones from other cultures. As Leprechauns, they express the Elemental characteristics of living interdimensionally, with a strong connection to nature. They also vacillate between being serious teachers and rowdy jokesters. They'll lecture you one minute, and then tickle you the next.

Even though we think of Leprechauns as red-bearded little men with paunches and green outfits, the members of the Leprechaun realm can look as gorgeous as fashion models. Many members of this realm do have touches of Leprechaun looks, whether it's a penchant for wearing green T-shirts, reddish hair, a ruddy complexion, or even a bit of a tummy paunch.

Leprechauns make wonderfully entertaining teachers who keep their students interested. They're skilled storytellers, yet their tales always have important messages. As long as you can weather their vacillating moods and occasional flirtations, Leprechauns make wonderful friends and romantic partners. You'll never be bored with a member of this realm, that's for sure!

Life Purpose and Career

With their penchant for storytelling and entertaining, Leprechauns make wonderful teachers who enthrall their students and make the lessons come alive. Leprechauns, with their Elemental heritage, have an innate sense of timing; they tell great jokes and know exactly when to emphasize phrases and words as they teach. With their childlike nature, Leprechauns can teach both children and adults. They reach deeply into children's psyches and the inner children of adult students.

Leprechauns also excel in the arts and entertainment industries. They cherish the variety that these fields offer, as they can easily grow bored. Leprechauns appreciate—and conquer—challenges.

In Relationships

Leprechauns are very attractive romantic partners because of their keen sense of humor and playfulness. People fall in love with Leprechauns, because they make others laugh and feel at ease and childlike. Yet, a few months into the relationship, the romantic partner may complain that the Leprechaun is immature and irresponsible. For that reason, Leprechauns do best being in romantic relationships with other Elemental-based realms. Both partners can feel free to be silly and childlike without fear of offending each other. Leprechauns are prone to alcoholism and substance abuse, which can negatively affect relationships. Meditation, creative projects, regular exercise, talk therapy, and 12-step programs can help Leprechauns channel their addictive side into constructive pursuits.

CHAPTER TWELVE

MERPEOPLE

You may be a Merperson if you:

- Must live near the ocean or a lake in order to feel sane and happy

- Are deeply concerned with the health of the world's oceans

- Do volunteer and activism work to protect the oceans, dolphins, whales, and other marine creatures

- Always have a bottle or glass of water in your hands

- Suffer from dry skin and/or constipation

- Feel cold, even in warm weather

- Love the tropics
- Are obsessed with mermaids
- Are a woman with a curvy figure
- Love to swim, and are very good at breath-holding
- Often wear ocean-colored clothing
- Have a green tint in your eyes
- Have red tones in your hair

> The majority of Merpeople have green coloring in their eyes.

Like Leprechauns, Merpeople are hybrids from the Elemental realm, so they also possess playful and mischievous sides. In my book *Mermaids 101*, I published the results of my survey of Merpeople:

I selected only the surveys of those who knew that they were definitely Merpeople. Most based this opinion on the fact that they matched my descriptions; they *had* to live near water, they'd identified with mermaids or mermen since childhood, they had frequent dreams about mermaids, and so on.

Of all the measures on the survey, the significant factors were:

- 82% had a natural red tint or highlights in their hair

- 82% preferred to wear their hair long (89% of just the females surveyed)

- 79% had naturally curly or wavy hair

- 69% had green in their eyes

- 85% reported being frequently or constantly thirsty

- 80% said they felt cold often, even in warm weather

The 82 percent of red- and auburn-haired respondents eclipses the estimated 2 to 10 percent of people with naturally red or auburn hair in the general population. Apparently, red hair is a genetic anomaly. At one time, red-haired women were accused of witchcraft. In the 16th and 17th centuries, redheaded European women were put to death during the witch-hunting crusades.

Could they have been Merpeople who retained their magical abilities and knowledge?

As mentioned above, Merpeople must live near bodies of water to feel happy and healthy. MerFairies are drawn to rivers and lakes, while MerAngels, Mystic Mers, MerCherubs, and Star-Mers feel connected to the ocean. Many Merpeople have memories of, or are attracted to stories about, Atlantis and Lemuria, which are two ancient oceanic civilizations.

As with other realms, Merpeople look like their spiritual counterparts. Female Merpeople resemble mermaids, with hourglass, curvy figures and a penchant for wearing turquoise or water-colored clothing. Mermen look athletic, trim, and outdoorsy. Both genders prefer wearing their hair long, and their tresses have natural waves. The majority have a naturally red tint in their hair.

Merpeople report feeling cold easily, and they prefer to vacation or live in tropical climates. As much as they love to swim, though, Merpeople avoid chlorinated pools because they're sensitive to the smell and feel of chlorine.

Merpeople are frequently thirsty, and many have issues with constipation. They usually have a bottle of water at hand, and they do best avoiding dried fruit, which tends to leach water out of their systems. Their water sensitivity also causes Merpeople to be very choosy about which brand of bottled water they drink. Merpeople often crave seaweed salad, sea vegetables, and nori (flattened seaweed wrapped around sushi rolls), probably because their bodies need the special sea-based nutrients.

Most people love dolphins, but Merpeople are fanatical about them. They also love whales, seabirds, seahorses, and other water-dwelling beings. Many Merpeople volunteer time or money to support charities or events that protect the oceans, reefs, cetaceans, lakes, and rivers. Their favorite vacation destination is a tropical beach, and they either live near a body of water or long to do so. Merpeople also diligently pick up litter from beaches and lakefronts.

Life Purpose and Career

Merpeople took on human form in this lifetime in order to protect the world's water supply, the ocean, and her inhabitants. So regardless of their career choice, Merpeople must engage in activism related to protecting dolphins, whales, sea turtles, sharks, and the like. This could involve posting blogs and petitions, organizing or attending protest rallies, or participating in an ocean charity, such as Surfriders Foundation, Sea Shepherd, or Oceana.

Merpeople are happiest when they are near or on the water, so they enjoy careers such as oceanography, scuba instruction, leading dolphin-sighting excursions, and underwater photography. These days, many Merpeople are making careers out of wearing swimmable mermaid and merman tails and working at birthday parties and in television commercials. Some people make and sell mermaid tails and mermaid-related art and jewelry for a living. This is a topic I write about in my book *Mermaids 101*.

In Relationships

Merpeople are usually independent loners; it takes a special person to win the heart of a mermaid or merman. Merpeople are warm and friendly, but they've felt their share of betrayal, so they're also guarded and mistrustful. Merpeople can be "slippery fish" who swim quickly away from a relationship, without looking back. It may be awhile before a Merperson will drop his or her guard and have a deep connection with someone else. Patience is necessary to be in a relationship with a Merperson, but that patience is eventually greatly rewarded.

Different Types of Merpeople

There are several Merpeople subcategories, including:

MerAngels

As a hybrid of half Incarnated Angel and half Elemental (Mer is part of the Elemental realm), MerAngels vacillate between being naughty and nice. Female MerAngels may resemble Incarnated Angels, with their voluptuous bodies; heart-shaped youthful faces; and tumbling, highlighted hair. Yet, they are the Incarnated Angels who've lived on the edge. They may have histories of drug and alcohol abuse, relationship betrayals, and even criminal records. However, their hearts are purely angelic at the core.

MerFairies

This hybrid is 100 percent Elemental, so Mer-Fairies have no apologies about being party animals at the ocean, lakes, or rivers. They enjoy cocktails while watching seaside sunsets, boating, or lazing on a beach. MerFairies can be perfectionistic about their romantic partners, which may lead to a long succession of boyfriends and girlfriends. Yet, MerFairies will tell you that they're trying to find lifelong satisfaction, in the form of a fun, financially secure—oh, and did I mention *fun?*—relationship. MerFairies love to camp, hike, and be next to lakes and rivers set in the mountains. They have a special bond with the water fairies, which are called "sprites" and "undines."

MerCherubs

This hybrid is a combination Merperson and Cherub. More than any other Merperson variety, the MerCherub brushes her hair and reapplies makeup to a level of beautiful perfection. MerCherubs love swimming, as long as it doesn't mess up their hairstyle or makeup. In fact, MerCherubs love the water experience if it can be beautified with an attractive swimsuit or a swimmable mermaid tail.

Star-Mers

Starpeople enjoy being near the ocean, but this hybrid is especially drawn to the sea. Star-Mers are loners who prefer to sail, swim, surf, or snorkel by themselves (or with one special and trusted companion). Star-Mers especially love to look at the starry skies while drifting on a boat in the middle of the ocean. They connect with their home planets through the energy of the water's positive ions.

Mystic Mers

This hybrid realm is a blend of Merperson and Wise One. They have the edgy Elemental personality combined with the seriousness of Wise Ones. They love to teach, especially about dolphins, whales, Atlantis, ocean ecology, scuba diving, sailing, or any other wisdom related to the ocean. A subcategory of this realm, the Mystic MerAngel, is a blend of an Incarnated Angel, Merperson, and Wise One.

Incarnated Dolphins

This hybrid consists of dolphins who have taken on human form so that their message is clearly heard by people. Yet, their appearance reveals their true identity. Incarnated Dolphins' bodies are shaped like *actual* dolphin bodies. Their slightly protruding belly casts their body with the same dimensions as an American football.

Incarnated Dolphins also chuckle with the same snickering laugh of ocean-dwelling dolphins. Most Incarnated Dolphins have sea-related professions such as marine biologist, oceanographer, boat captain, or ocean ecologist. They're passionate about preserving the sea's ecosystem and make wonderful teachers in this area.

Because of their dolphin origin, those from this realm know how to relax, play, and flirt while meeting their responsibilities. Because they're accustomed to swimming in pods, Incarnated Dolphins are usually very social. They love long and lighthearted discussions. Incarnated Dolphins avoid any stressful work and are discerning about how they spend their time. After all, why struggle when it's so much more pleasant to relax and play?

A woman I know named Gayle loves dolphins, and regularly leads group excursions to swim with them in exotic locations. She even looks like a dolphin, with her sleekly rounded body and oval eyes. Interestingly, Gayle runs a swimming-pool company. Her sun sign is Pisces, the fish, and a water sign. She says, "I love the ocean and *have* to spend time there to recharge. I love dolphins and whales and spend much time in the ocean swimming with them. I asked my guides why I feel so connected to the ocean, and I was told, 'Because, Gayle, you are *of* the ocean.' At first, I didn't understand what that meant. Now I do believe that I may have been a dolphin before."

In addition to Incarnated Dolphins, I've also met a few Incarnated Whales—and, no, they're not obese.

Most Incarnated Dolphins have gray eyes, like their oceanic counterparts.

Life Purpose and Career

While Incarnated Dolphins have a playful, Elemental personality, Incarnated Whales have the protective and loving energy of archangels. Incarnated

Whales are fascinated with sea-dwelling whales; and often become advocates, activists, marine biologists, sailors, or scuba divers in order to spend time studying whales.

Because Incarnated Dolphins dislike hard work or stress, they are often criticized as being "lazy." They're really not lazy, though. If a project truly calls to them, they will throw their efforts in that direction. But they will also balance work with lots of time for rest and play, because those are high priorities to the Incarnated Dolphin.

In Relationships

Incarnated Dolphins are very affectionate, and their lucky partners will feel very loved and nurtured. The only issues that arise are because Incarnated Dolphins dislike housework, so their partners, family members, and roommates may complain about the disorganized work and living environment. Fortunately, the easygoing Dolphin isn't quickly offended and may take another nap or engage in playful activities as a stress reliever.

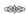

These are the major hybrids that have been revealed to me since teaching this material to audience members. Those who can't relate to any of the realms continue to help me pinpoint other hybrids. Yet, some people just defy all realm categories. For them, we've developed other ways of looking at blended realms, as you'll read about next.

CHAPTER THIRTEEN

IF YOU FEEL THAT YOU FIT INTO SEVERAL REALMS . . .

About 10 percent of my audience members who hear the descriptions of the Earth Angel realms tell me, "I feel like I fit into more than one category!" These Earth Angels are unclear about their particular realm. Here are some points to consider:

1. Energy: Tune in to your overall "energy blueprint"

The energy of a(n):	Is:
Incarnated Angel	Sweet and loving
Incarnated Elemental	Warm, playful, and mischievous
Flower Fairy	Sweet and shy
Forest Fairy	Sweet and intense
Star Fairy	Sweet and socially awkward
Starperson	Helpful, cool, and detached
Wise One	Serious, intense, and regal
Mystic Angel	Serious, intense, sweet, and loving
Knight Paladin and Galactic Knight	Attentive and polite, yet socially awkward
Aladdin Genie	Adventurous, humorous, and generous
Atlantean	Elegant and classy
Incarnated Cherub	Romantic
Mystic Star and Cosmic Angel	Socially awkward, yet kind and helpful
Leprechaun	Alternately serious and silly
Merperson	Alternately rebellious and acquiescent
Incarnated Dolphin	Easygoing and lighthearted

2. Physical appearance	
People in this realm:	**Have these physical characteristics:**
Incarnated Angel	Beautiful or cherubic faces with large bodies
Incarnated Elemental	Look like larger versions of fairies, elves, sprites, and gnomes
Flower Fairy	Very tiny and petite, with an attractive face and clear complexion
Forest Fairy	Thin, with a Celtic appearance (reddish hair, freckles)
Star Fairy	Tall, heavyset, and large boned. They wear little makeup and dress eccentrically.
Starperson	Tall and lanky; or short, with thin or large bodies. They have unusual eyes and facial features. Plain in dress, they wear minimal makeup.
Wise One	Long faces, with faraway expressions in their eyes. They wear dark-colored flowing shirts and dresses and often have long, prematurely gray hair.
Mystic Angel	An attractive face, large body, thick dark hair, and a serious facial expression
Knight Paladin and Galactic Knight	Tall, large body, intense eyes, posture is at attention

Aladdin Genie	Thin and often petite; they dress in light fabrics and often revealing or body-conscious clothing. They love to wear sparkly clothing accents and jewelry.
Atlantean	Perfect and stately posture; long, dark hair; usually dark skin and eyes. They often dress in Grecian-inspired clothing.
Incarnated Cherub	Heart-shaped face; long, healthy dark hair that is well groomed and styled; fancy clothing and jewelry; heavy makeup; manicured nails; small mouth with large, pouty lips. Often petite, but some Cherubs are tall.
Mystic Star and Cosmic Angel	Tall to medium height; thin; and long, straight hair. Little to no makeup, and clothing for practicality instead of visibility.
Leprechaun	Many look like leprechauns, with a Celtic appearance of reddish hair, ruddy complexion, and freckles. They prefer to wear green and earth-tone–colored clothing. They have a twinkle in their eyes most of the time.
Merperson	Females have hourglass-like curvy bodies. Eyes tend to have green in them, and hair tends to have red in it. Male and female Merpeople prefer long hair. They often wear blue-, turquoise-, or teal-colored clothing.
Incarnated Dolphin	Gray or blue eyes, large stomach that gives their bodies a dolphin-like appearance.

3. Interests	
People in this realm:	**Focus on:**
Incarnated Angel	Healing and service work; keeping relationships peaceful and happy
Incarnated Elemental	Teaching, entertaining, the arts, and environmentalism
Flower Fairy	Flowers
Forest Fairy	Trees
Star Fairy	Unusual flowers
Starperson	Energy healing, particularly Reiki; technological advances; being helpful as needed
Wise One	Teaching; practicing mystical, psychic, and Earth-based spirituality
Mystic Angel	Teaching about healing
Knight Paladin and Galactic Knight	Upholding justice, truth, and freedom; protecting "underdogs" and just causes
Aladdin Genie	Music, dance, storytelling, spicy food, deserts, and mountains
Atlantean	Learning about and teaching esoteric wisdom and a focus on returning the planet to natural energy sources (such as solar, wind, and tidal)

Incarnated Cherub	Romance and beauty
Mystic Star and Cosmic Angel	Creating peace on Earth
Leprechaun	Teaching, music, storytelling, playing practical jokes
Merperson	Dolphins, whales, water sports, the ocean, and other bodies of water
Incarnated Dolphin	Dolphins, resting, playing

The Evolving Soul and the Shape-shifter

If you still don't know your realm, you may come from an as-yet-undiscovered realm. Or you may be an "Evolving Soul" or a "Shape-shifter." (We previously called the Shape-shifter group by the term *Dabblers*). That means that you're either moving from one realm to the next, or are hopscotching through the realms for the sake of variety and growth.

The Evolving Soul

If you're an Evolving Soul, you're moving from one realm to the next, so you may not identify with one particular group. Perhaps you've spent many lifetimes in one realm and have learned everything you can from this experience, so you elect to enter a new realm. You don't identify fully with the group you just left or the group you're newly joining.

If this sounds like you, give yourself time to adjust to the new group, and don't judge yourself harshly for feeling disconnected. Earth Angels in the Evolving Soul category can feel doubly alienated—not only do you feel separate from humans, but you feel different from the other Earth Angels as well! It can feel like being the last kid picked for a softball team: unwanted and unappreciated.

Know that these are temporary feelings, and pray for spiritual assistance to know that you're not alone and that you *are* wanted and appreciated. After all, you were very brave to switch to a new realm, and you probably did so out of the noble intention to be extra helpful to the world!

The Shape-shifter

Some souls desire variety, excitement, and a wealth of experience. If you're a Shape-shifter, like "a kid in a candy store," you can't decide what you want, so you select everything on the menu. The Shape-shifters are Earth Angels who move from realm to realm. You never quite settle into one particular realm family. Instead, you graze from the highlights that each realm has to offer. Simultaneously, you bring gifts to each realm from the lessons you've learned while in the other Earth Angel realms. Shape-shifters rapidly adapt to new situations and people, much like children who move a lot and attend different schools, yet develop the ability to quickly fit in.

If you're an Evolving Soul or a Shape-shifter, you're like a honeybee going from flower to flower, taking and bringing nourishment as you travel. You provide valuable services because you infuse the realms with fresh blood, new ideas, and awakened vitality.

You could also be from a new realm that's yet undiscovered. As the world unfolds, new missions are required. And if you're one of the souls initiating those new missions, God bless you for your service!

Life-Path Work for Evolving Souls and Shape-shifters

Evolving Souls and Shape-shifters fall into two distinct groups: the Independent Thinkers and the

Adapters. Independent Thinkers are take-charge individuals and radical nonconformists who pride themselves on being outsiders. They believe that "normalcy" is tantamount to being sentenced to mediocrity. Independent Thinkers are champions of humanitarian and environmentalist causes—unless the causes are too popular. Independent Thinkers don't like to be trendy, and they desire their own unique niche outside of the mass populace.

Independent Thinkers, not surprisingly, do best in self-employment work revolving around artistic or inventive pursuits. They don't enjoy systems, rules, or guidelines from outside "authorities." Ideal careers for Independent Thinkers would be the fine arts, craftwork, publishing, writing, or photography.

Shape-shifters love any career that offers them excitement and an opportunity to learn. They're more comfortable working with the public than the Independent Thinkers. Ideal careers would be travel (working as a tour guide or working on a cruise ship), being a talent agent or scout (making other people's dreams come true), and any sales work involving a product or service that the Shape-shifter truly believes in.

Guidance and Suggestions If You're an Evolving Soul or a Shape-shifter

— *Respect your decision for independence.* Souls in this nonrealm are generally nonconformists and rabble-rousers. The earth needs your strength and power right now, so please don't dilute it by trying to fit into any particular group (unless it comes naturally).

— *Teach freedom.* Too many humans allow themselves to be controlled by reigning authorities. By your refusal to conform or be tied down, you teach them alternatives. The more you can do to garner personal happiness and peace, the more effective your teachings will be. Remember that you teach first by example, and then formal teaching opportunities arise as you allow them.

— *Manifest, manifest, manifest.* Because you tend to work outside of systems, you need to rely upon your personal manifestation power to sustain you materially. Remember that there are no neutral thoughts or words, so everything you say and think creates your future. Therefore, think about what you desire, not about what you fear.

AFTERWORD

WE'RE COUNTING ON YOU!

Earth Angel, thank you for being on the planet at this time. With your great loving energy, you're helping us just by being here! And yet—as you're well aware—you signed up for so much more. You elected to come here at a crucial time in our planet's history to effect great change, utilizing your natural resources of talents combined with harmonious actions.

Unless the mass populace takes a different approach to the environment and each other, life as we know it may not continue. You're here to teach alternatives. You'll know what to teach by noticing which issues fuel your passions, excitement, worry, or anger. For example, you might be here to teach us, your fellow human beings, how to manifest material needs so that we don't compete, steal, or go to war to get our share. Or perhaps you're here to teach about the vital necessity of protecting our air, water, and soil quality. Maybe it's in your soul contract to teach healthier ways to raise and educate children. There are hundreds of vital topics to teach right now.

How do you teach? Any way that you can—for instance, by being a role model, authoring books and articles, sending letters to editors of publications, posting and signing petitions on social media sites, organizing or attending peaceful rallies, boycotting, taking action within educational and government systems, and/or giving speeches or making media appearances.

One thing is clear: We need Earth Angels who are willing to be leaders. Old systems that lack integrity are beginning to fall, such as corporations and churches with histories of abuse. The new energy will no longer support or hide dark energy. Darkness within the educational, government, and legal systems will also cause them to wobble. As these changes occur, Earth Angel leaders (such as you) can guide people away from panic and pessimism, and toward a focus on letting the old be replaced with something better.

We're all counting on you to take the reins of your life purpose and embrace it fully. Any step that you take is helpful and sorely needed right now . . . provided that it comes from your intention to help.

Please don't delay moving forward, waiting to figure out exactly what your mission is or what next step to take, or to receive an ironclad guarantee that you'll succeed. Doing *anything* that comes from love in your heart will be helpful, much like the ways in which small gifts given to a worthy cause eventually add up to a hefty donation. Start anywhere—just dive in!

Along the way, please take good care of your physical body. It's a very important tool in your mission. Yet, you, like many Earth Angels may have never had a physical human body before, so you may neglect or abuse it. By feeding it organic foods and beverages, exercising regularly, detoxing, and getting adequate rest, you'll have more energy for your life purpose.

A number of years ago, a very influential Earth Angel named Louise Hay (who's the founder of Hay House, my publisher) was guided to write about her insights into the link between physical ailments and underlying thoughts. Yet, not one publisher would print her materials! So instead of giving up, she typed and stapled several copies of the manuscript herself. Then, she felt urged to give workshops on the topic. At first, only two or three people came to her lectures. Today, her manuscript—*Heal Your Body*—has helped countless people, and was the basis for her *New York Times* bestseller *You Can Heal Your Life,* which has sold

50 million copies around the world. And now, when Louise gives a lecture, thousands of people attend!

Aren't you glad that Louise didn't get discouraged about her life purpose and that she persevered? There are dozens of similar stories of people who've made the world a better place, and whose beginnings were quite humble.

⊰✣⊱

Your true self is a creation of love, while your ego is a creation of fear. Your ego's goals are aimed toward making you feel small, inadequate, and powerless, yet how can a being who's made in the image and likeness of the Creator be *anything* but mighty, powerful, and wise?

Your ego knows that if you remember your true spiritual nature (perfect, powerful, creative, and intelligent), it will lose its power to frighten you, so it feeds you lies such as: "If you become powerful, you'll abuse that power. People won't like you as much. People will be jealous of you," and so on. Please, please don't listen to the ego! Tell it to go sit in the corner and keep its rantings to itself. Treat it like a buzzing fly, and don't focus on it.

The angels say, "If you get nervous, focus on service." Nervousness comes from ego concerns about other people's opinions. A focus on "How can I bring more love and light to this situation right now?" elicits your higher self's natural spiritual gifts and power.

Remember that the bigger the purpose, the bigger the fear; there's a correlation. The more people you'll potentially help, the more force your ego will use to hold you back. Your ego urges you to delay your mission by preparing instead of doing. Your ego says, "First you have to lose weight, make more money, get married, get divorced, move, graduate, get published, open a healing center, and so forth . . . and *then* you'll be able to help the world." That's nonsense!

Earth Angel, you're ready right now for your mission! There will never be a day more perfect than today to work on it! Even though you may feel unqualified or unprepared, do it anyway! Author Sheldon Kopp once wrote: "I have never begun any important venture for which I felt adequately prepared." In other words, you'll probably never feel completely ready for your mission, so there's no point in waiting.

Pray for daily assignments that tell you how you can help make Earth a cleaner and more peaceful environment. Your prayers will be answered in the form of opportunities for you to teach and heal. As these doors open for you, please don't turn and run the other way. You *are* ready. You *deserve* to do this beautiful work. And you *are* qualified . . . *now!*

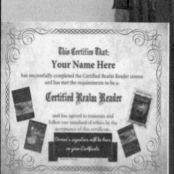

ABOUT THE
AUTHOR

Doreen Virtue holds B.A., M.A., and Ph.D. degrees in counseling psychology. A former psychotherapist, Doreen now gives workshops on topics related to her books and oracle cards. She's the author of *Assertiveness for Earth Angels, How to Hear Your Angels,* and *Angel Tarot Cards,* among many other books and oracle card decks. She has appeared on *Oprah,* CNN, and *Good Morning America;* and has been featured in newspapers and magazines worldwide. For information on Doreen's work, please visit her at AngelTherapy.com or facebook.com/DoreenVirtue444. To enroll in Doreen's online video course and become a Certified Realm Reader who helps people understand their Earth Angel realm, please visit www.RealmReader.com.

NOTES

NOTES

NOTES

NOTES

NOTES

Hay House Titles of Related Interest

YOU CAN HEAL YOUR LIFE, the movie,
starring Louise Hay & Friends
(available as a 1-DVD program and an expanded 2-DVD set)
Watch the trailer at: www.LouiseHayMovie.com

THE SHIFT, the movie,
starring Dr. Wayne W. Dyer
(available as a 1-DVD program and an expanded 2-DVD set)
Watch the trailer at: www.DyerMovie.com

❧

*ADVENTURES OF THE SOUL: Journeys Through the Physical
and Spiritual Dimensions,* by James Van Praagh

*THE EARTH DIET: Your Complete Guide to Living Using Earth's
Natural Ingredients,* by Liana Werner-Gray

*THE LAW OF ATTRACTION: The Basics of the Teachings
of Abraham®,* by Esther and Jerry Hicks

*MEDITATION: Achieving Inner Peace and Tranquility
in Your Life,* by Brian L. Weiss, M.D.

MINDFUL INTENTIONS,
by Louie Schwartzberg and Miraval (book-with-DVD)

*REAL FOOD REVOLUTION: Healthy Eating, Green Groceries,
and the Return of the American Family Farm,*
by Congressman Tim Ryan

All of the above are available at your local bookstore,
or may be ordered by contacting Hay House (see next page).

We hope you enjoyed this Hay House book. If you'd like to receive our online catalog featuring additional information on Hay House books and products, or if you'd like to find out more about the Hay Foundation, please contact:

Hay House, Inc., P.O. Box 5100, Carlsbad, CA 92018-5100
(760) 431-7695 or (800) 654-5126
(760) 431-6948 (fax) or (800) 650-5115 (fax)
www.hayhouse.com® • www.hayfoundation.org

Published and distributed in Australia by:
Hay House Australia Pty. Ltd., 18/36 Ralph St., Alexandria
NSW 2015 • *Phone:* 612-9669-4299 • *Fax:* 612-9669-4144
www.hayhouse.com.au

Published and distributed in the United Kingdom by:
Hay House UK, Ltd., Astley House, 33 Notting Hill Gate, London
W11 3JQ • *Phone:* 44-20-3675-2450 • *Fax:* 44-20-3675-2451
www.hayhouse.co.uk

Published and distributed in the Republic of South Africa by:
Hay House SA (Pty), Ltd., P.O. Box 990, Witkoppen 2068
Phone/Fax: 27-11-467-8904 • www.hayhouse.co.za

Published in India by: Hay House Publishers India, Muskaan
Complex, Plot No. 3, B-2, Vasant Kunj, New Delhi 110 070
Phone: 91-11-4176-1620 • *Fax:* 91-11-4176-1630
www.hayhouse.co.in

Distributed in Canada by: Raincoast Books, 2440 Viking
Way, Richmond, B.C. V6V 1N2 • *Phone:* 1-800-663-5714
Fax: 1-800-565-3770 • www.raincoast.com

Take Your Soul on a Vacation

Visit www.HealYourLife.com® to regroup, recharge, and reconnect with your own magnificence. Featuring blogs, mind-body-spirit news, and life-changing wisdom from Louise Hay and friends.

Visit www.HealYourLife.com today!